On Thinking

GILBERT RYLE

On Thinking

edited by Konstantin Kolenda
with an Introduction by G. J. Warnock

**ROWMAN AND LITTLEFIELD
TOTOWA, NEW JERSEY**

First published in the United States 1979

Library of Congress Cataloging in Publication Data

Ryle, Gilbert, 1900–
  On thinking.
    1. Thought and thinking.   I. Kolenda, Konstantin.
  II. Title.
BF455.R94   153.4′2   79–16519

ISBN 0–8476–6203–9

Printed in Great Britain

CONTENTS

ACKNOWLEDGEMENTS

Chapter 4, 'Thinking and Self-Teaching', and Chapter 5, 'Thinking and Saying', and the Appendix, 'On Bouwsma's Wittgenstein', have been reprinted from *Rice University Studies*, Vol. 58, No. 3, Summer 1972, by permission of the editors. Chapter 6, 'Mowgli in Babel', has been reprinted from *Philosophy*, Vol. 49, No. 187, January 1974; Chapter 7, 'Negative Actions', has been reprinted from *Hermathena*, No. CXV, Summer 1973; and Chapter 8, 'Improvisation', has been reprinted from *Mind*, Vol. LXXXV, No. 337, January 1976, all by permission of the editors.

PREFACE

It is a privilege to have been asked to write a prefatory page or two on this collection of Gilbert Ryle's thoughts about Thinking. Professor Kolenda is, I think, absolutely right in believing that these late papers of Ryle's deserve to be thus brought and kept together, and philosophers will be grateful to him for making that possible. Ryle was in general highly critical of what one might call the *Nachlass*-business, I think for two reasons. One was that he felt that a philosopher – any writer, perhaps – was entitled to decide for himself which, and how much, of his writings should go on public record, and that it was, in a way, an improper use of a writer's property, and an invasion of his privacy, to take out of his desk (or waste-paper basket) after his death, and to print, items which their owner might have decided, and might even in some cases be known to have decided, should not be printed. The other reason was, I believe, that the posthumous scraping of literary barrels is liable to take place in an atmosphere of reverent solemnity such as Ryle, at all times, thought both unbearable and, usually, damaging. But neither ground for hesitation is pertinent in this case. Ryle's own writings pretty conclusively inhibit reverent solemnity; and, though the papers collected here would no doubt not have appeared unmodified in the book on thinking which Ryle, up to the time of his death in 1976, still had in view, they were all intended, and were actually used, for public presentation in one way or another. They did not go into, and have not been fished out of, his waste-paper basket.

It happens that I can add, and may perhaps be allowed this prefatory opportunity of adding, a sort of little footnote to *The Concept of Mind* which, small though it admittedly is, may be of interest. In the very early 1950s a seminar was held in Oxford entirely devoted, once a week for one term, to discussions of that recently-published book. Ryle, who used to say that he was no authority on the exposition or explanation of that work, came to one or two of these meetings, but was more often not there. It fell to me to read a paper to this seminar on Chapter V – 'Dispositions and Occurrences'. Ryle was not present when I read the paper, but rather to my alarm (I was a nervous young man at the time), he asked me afterwards if he might look at it. He returned it to me in due course with some marginal comments, and these seem to me to be of some modest interest.

I said first that the contrast between the 'occurrences' and 'dispositions' seemed to me, in Ryle's book, to *look* more important to him than it really was. The supposed distinction sometimes looked as if it were absolutely crucial to a bold and sweeping general thesis. 'The impression', I wrote, 'that one sometimes collects from his pages, or certainly that one is given by his unwary supporters, is that he wishes to deny that there are any happenings at all to be rightly called 'mental', and so to assert that to speak of a person's mind is always to speak ('dispositionally') of certain occurrences, overt doings and undergoings, which tend, are apt or likely or liable (etc.) to occur, in a single, well-illuminated public world. No statements about minds would be, in his adopted terminology, categorical; none would state facts; the only true categorical statements would be those stating facts about overt physical happenings.' If that were the case to be argued – and certainly some of Ryle's readers seem to think, whether admiringly of accusingly, that it was – then to establish firmly a distinction between 'occurrences' and 'dispositions', and in parallel between 'categorical' and 'hypothetical' propositions, would be of central importance. But, I said, perhaps this distinction was not really so important, since Ryle 'does not, or does not often, argue this case'.

Ryle commented on this: 'Yes. When I wrote the first draft it weighed with me much too much. I was getting more tepid about it before the end, but certainly one of my feet was still pretty firmly encased in this boot.'

A couple of pages later I wrote (the point being pretty obvious) that part of Ryle's reason for saying that, for instance, 'Brown is enjoying his work in the garden' does not 'signify an occurrence' was that, in such a case, the relation of enjoying to working was not just that of two concomitant activities, working and enjoying, going on at the same time. ('Could one be occupied simply in enjoying, without tiring oneself by doing something else as well?') Ryle's highly characteristic comment was: 'Yes, this is what I was tilting *against* – the idea that something mental was happening as the effect (or cause or concomitant) of something physical which was also happening. But – as always – the demolition programme produced its own dust-clouds.'

My more general point was that, in or in close proximity to his distinction between 'occurrences' and 'dispositions', Ryle seemed to me to be often relying upon, and only very inadequately qualifying, a supposed distinction which he characterized in various ways – in a logical-looking way as that between 'categorical' and 'hypothetical' propositions; less formally, as that between 'narrating' and 'explaining', or 'reporting' and 'predicting'; and in other ways too. Consider the qualification that he introduced. There are – and, he seemed to imply, there are a *few* – things that we say that he classified, slightly pejoratively, as 'mongrel-categorical'; they require for their truth that something be currently going on, but not only that – they require also that something regularly does go on, or that what is going on should have a particular actual or intended outcome, or something of that (not immediately present) sort. Take the sentence 'That bird is migrating'. If it is to be true that that bird is migrating, then it must be currently the case that that bird is flying (say) south; but it must also be true that that bird is a migrant, that is, belongs to a species whose members regularly migrate, and that its current flight will actually take it to (say) North Africa for the winter, rather than briefly into the next field or county or back to its nest. But on either side of these mongrels, Ryle's text seemed to imply, there are 'pure' categoricals, true narrations or reports of episodes or occurrences, and 'pure' hypotheticals, merely predicting or explaining, or stating regularities or propensities.

'But,' I wrote, 'there is no need at all to search for examples that have one foot on each side of this distinction – they are, particularly in our discourse about people, quite embarrassingly common. We are after all constantly concerned with the reasons, motives, and results of human conduct; and thus it is an enormously common thing for our reports of what people are doing to be coloured by our hopes and fears, guesses and

assumptions, about their reasons and motives and the probable
or intended outcome. So common, indeed, is this that one of the
most ordinary ways of asking for an *explanation* of someone's
behaviour is to ask the question: what is he doing? . . . . We shall say
that we know *what* he is doing when we know *why* he is (for
example) waving those flags – he is signalling, his intention is
to send a message. Compare "He is running away" – he hopes to
escape. "He is setting his watch" – he wants it to record the
correct time. "He is arranging his books" – he wants them to be in
a certain order. "He is digging a grave" – a corpse will be de-
posited in that hole. . . . Isn't "He is walking", even, a mongrel, by
contrast with "His legs are moving"? and isn't this a general
case?'

With this Ryle enthusiastically agreed. On my remark that,
'particularly in our discourse about people', what Ryle called
'mongrel-categoricals' were not exceptional, he commented: 'I
now think that it is almost analytic to say that they are the rule.
Roughly, that's what people are – i.e. (roughly) that's what
shape talk about people has'. And on the next page he wanted
to make the point more generally than I had. I had said that
'events in which only inanimate objects are involved, or perhaps
such things as goldfish or bacteria, might well be described in
purely episodic terms. . . .' 'No,' said Ryle, 'only relatively, in
comparison with more heavily loaded talk.' And on my remark
that 'so long as we continue to talk about people, we never reach
the episodic ground-floor,' he wrote: 'I agree, and would go
further. We never reach it in talk about birds or clouds either.
Biological talk about people is *relatively* non-"mongrell", but
biological talk about people and lizards is highly "mongrel" *relatively* to kinetic or electric talk about them.' On the suggestion
that so common a case should not be called 'mongrel', he noted:
'Yes. It amuses me now to remember that I then thought I was
being very daring and naughty in venturing to insert just a few
greys between the official Blacks and Whites.' I ended by saying
that 'we must not be occurrence-disposition Dualists. There is a
very large piece of territory in between.' This drew the wonder-
fully typical comment: 'Yes, indeed! In fact the North and South
poles really occupy no territory at all. They can't be colonized,
though colonizers need to know the difference between North
and South. (But even this picture suggests an ultimate bi-
polarity, which stinks a bit.)'

I believe that these few comments may be of some interest, not just as being Ryle's and highly characteristic of Ryle. One thing that they show is that one very crude version of the alleged mind-body 'category mistake' – that what were taken to be categorical propositions about mental happenings were *really* hypothetical propositions about physical happenings – not only had at one time been in Ryle's mind, but still does (as many have suspected) occasionally break surface in the book as we have it – 'one of my feet was still pretty firmly encased in this boot'. The other thing that they seem to me to show is how early, and how explicitly, Ryle had given up the idea of seeking philosophical health through any definite programme of correct assignments to definite, well-regimented 'categories'. The implication of some of his comments seems to be that there are not two kinds, or five kinds, or fifty kinds of things that we say, such that each thing that we say could in principle be assigned once and for all to its appropriate kind; there is rather a continuum (many continua) of resemblances and differences, in which dicta can be appropriately (for certain purposes) located relatively to others. This, I suppose, is not the sort of position which his own terminology of 'categories' would naturally suggest, and thus perhaps any evidence is useful that Ryle did not, or at any rate not for long, seriously hold that he could tell us exactly what categories there are, and what belonged in each of them.

I have mentioned one impression that may be derived – and not altogether unreasonably derived – from a reading of *The Concept of Mind*: that the author seeks to reject altogether the notion of an 'inner life', to hold that *nothing* really happens inwardly, privately, in the mind alone – that everything that really occurs occurs publicly, unmysteriously, in the openly observable physical world, and is in principle fully and equally accessible to anybody and everybody. It used sometimes to be said of Ryle that at least part of the reason why he was inclined to espouse, at any rate not to reject as an obvious absurdity, this extraordinary doctrine might be that it was actually true of himself – that he *had* no 'inner life', and did not find it odd to deny the very existence of phenomena of which he actually had no first-hand experience. Well, that was a sort of witticism, no doubt meant to be no more. I am inclined to say, nevertheless, that it was quite profoundly untrue – not merely in the trivial sense that such an allegation could not really be true of anybody, but that in his case it would be quite exceptionally wide of the mark. It is true that the picture of life within whose terms he appeared to operate, and which to some extent may be drawn from his philosophical writings (which of course were not *intended* to present any such thing), is one of great simplicity, openness, ordinariness – of life lived very much on the surface, without secrets or mysteries or much propensity to move or to surprise, in which the round of honest work is diversified by jokes and games, unintrospective, undramatic, unpretentious, friendly. It would be a flat mistake, however, to take this picture as expressing Ryle's belief that life – whether his own or other people's – actually had this plain, depthless quality. I do not know that it either expresses or betrays even the slightest wish on his part that life should be like that. What is at issue, I believe, is not an absurd or idiosyncratic view of what life is like, but a view – perhaps idiosyncratic, but not absurd – as to how it should be decently conducted. We all present to other people, for the purposes of social life, versions of ourselves usually a good deal simplified, and edited certainly. Ryle was an outstandingly friendly, sociable, and (a word that particularly fits him) clubbable man; but I believe that he felt it proper, both for himself and others, to edit the public version, the version for the social uses of everyday, more austerely, more stoically, less self-indulgently and much more reticently than is usually done. He had views – old fashioned views, no doubt – about the desirable decencies of human relations. Just as he thought it right and important that a writer should decide what versions (literally) of his work should be part of the public record, so, I believe, he thought it right and important that each of us should decide what version (metaphorically) of ourselves we wished to be visible and made available to others. That he preferred, both for himself and others, a fairly simple version, as little as possible demanding, or oppressive, or *difficile*, was a question of manners not of metaphysical or any other high species of belief.

Ryle was an unusually tolerant, uncensorious person. He liked people on the whole, some less than others, but he did not demand or expect too much of anybody, and had no inclination to draw a line between the saved and the damned. He held naturally, I think, what he calls in one of his papers 'the Aristotelian pattern of ethical ideas,' which he found also in his favourite prose writer, Jane Austen – a pattern that represents 'people as differing from one another in degree and not in kind, and differing from one another not in respect just of a single generic Sunday attribute, Goodness, say, or else Wickedness, but in respect of a whole spectrum of specific week-day attributes. . . . A person is not black or white, but iridescent with all the colours of the rainbow; and he is not a flat plane, but a highly irregular solid. He is not blankly Good or Bad, blankly angelic or fiendish; he is better than most in one respect, about level with the average in another respect, and a bit, perhaps a big bit, deficient in a third respect. In fact he is like the people we really know. . . .' But if for Ryle persons were not black or white, the things that they did – and the distinction is entirely Aristotelian – occasionally were. In fifteen years as his colleague at Magdalen, I remember only two occasions when he forcefully intervened in the conduct of the college's business (during much of which, in fact, he was prone, very sensibly, to sleep). On the first occasion what was at issue, as he saw it, was justice; on the second occasion what was at issue was truthfulness. He could be, and on those occasions was, very formidable indeed.

HERTFORD COLLEGE, OXFORD   G. J. WARNOCK

INTRODUCTION

Anyone acquainted with Gilbert Ryle's *Concept of Mind* should find these essays worth reading. They are not peripheral to his main work, not an afterthought. They testify to Ryle's constant effort to sharpen his central philosophical position. Written during the last years of his life, these essays concentrate on what struck him as a most difficult and recalcitrant topic: thinking. That this topic should engage him in this persistent way is not surprising. After all, in his major work he undertook to provide not only a criticism of received philosophical accounts of the nature of the human mind, but also an alternative positive statement of how we are to understand this unique feature of ourselves. To the very end of his life he felt that his positive account needed strengthening.

Ryle's basic move is well, even notoriously, known. He inveighed repeatedly against a twin mistake: to put the concept of mind into either a mechanistic (Behaviourist) or a ghostly (Cartesian) framework. According to him, under the influence of some key figures in our philosophical tradition we tend to fall into one of the two conceptual pitfalls, which Ryle labeled Reductionism and Duplicationism: either we reduce the human mind to something less than it is, or we create for it a duplicate home in a disembodied superstructure. Both moves distort what we, in our bones, know the mind to be, and Ryle undertook the task of reminding us of what we, *pace* Behaviourist or Cartesian distortions, are perfectly familiar with.

As Ryle occasionally reminded his interpreters, his analysis of the mind was motivated by a more general discovery about the nature of philosophical problems. Early in his career he was attracted to arguments – Russell's, Moore's, Wittgenstein's – that showed how inattention to our conceptual geography tends to

1

generate nonsensical conclusions.[1] In his *Dilemmas* he considers several other intellectual troubles that result when 'theorists of one kind may unwittingly commit themselves to propositions belonging to quite another province of thinking,'[2] and many articles in the two volumes of his *Collected Papers* undertake the exposure of categorially disguised nonsense.

To inveigh against nonsense is of course to be concerned about our intellectual health; hence Ryle's care that we should not commit ourselves to nonsensical theories about the human mind. In most of his philosophical writings he was concerned to reveal the many ways in which our postulation of hidden or ethereal 'mental processes' leads us down the primrose path of paradox. But he was also keenly aware of another factor responsible for philosophical confusion: the failure to recognize that all our concepts tend to come in interrelated clusters. To introduce order and understanding into our theories we often must explore the entire relevant territory and deal with several neighbouring concepts at once.[3]

Not surprisingly, the same requirement must be met when our objective is not just to disentangle a mass of conceptual brambles, but also to produce a positive account of any important aspect of experience. This turns out to be the condition that Ryle tries to meet when he examines the concept of thinking. It became increasingly clear to him that in his main work he had neglected some of the topics that must be included in a satisfactory account of what it means to have a mind. He confessed in the Introduction to the second volume of *Collected Papers*, 'Also, like plenty of other people, I deplored the perfunctoriness with which *The Concept of Mind* had dealt with the Mind *qua* pensive. But I have latterly been concentrating heavily on this particular theme for the simple reason that it has turned out to be at once a still intractable and progressively ramifying maze.'[4] The essays in our collection are successive visits to this ramifying maze, and they examine in it many unexplored passages and connections. The result, I believe, adds new dimensions to Ryle's analysis of the concept of mind, although it is doubtful that he himself was wholly satisfied with the progress he made.[5] It is a pity that he did not live long enough to consolidate his thinking on thinking. Still, what he had said recently on this topic constitutes a considerable advance on what was said in *The Concept of Mind* and in some essays subsequently published in *Collected Papers*.

At this point it may be useful to provide a reminder of the general drift of Ryle's early positive account of the human mind. Most mental phenomena are competences acquired through learning, and they are to be distinguished from behaviour that is either instinctive or is established through mere drill. To develop intelligence we need training, in the process of which we learn *how* to do things. This knowledge involves governing our behaviour through mastered rules or techniques. The mastery of skills is manifested in dispositional, law-like capacities. Intelligent action is not caused by some hidden occult episodes but is shown forth in the character of the performance itself. That performance is heedful, in the sense that the agent knows what he is doing. He demonstrates that knowledge in his 'capacities, skills, habits, liabilities, and bents.'[6] To manifest a mastery of a skill one performance is not enough; 'a modest assemblage of heterogeneous performances' is required. Knowing how is not a single-track disposition like a reflex or a habit.

Among acquired dispositions is to be included the capacity traditionally recognized as characteristic of man as a rational animal, namely, the capacity to offer an argument. 'Having an argument, like having a pen, a theory or a plan, is different both from getting it and from using it. Using it entails having it and having it entails having got, and not lost it. But, unlike some sorts of theories and plans, arguments are not mastered merely by absorbing information, nor is mastery of them lost through shortnes of memory. They are more like skills.'[7] When a person uses an argument or draws a conclusion he produces, 'of course, a mental, indeed an intellectual act, since it is an exercise of one of those competences which are properly ranked as "intellectual".'[8]

Activities governed by dispositions acquired through learning and training entitle us to regard the agent as having a mind. Such dispositions exhibit a great variety and include the capacity to use abstract terms. But what characterizes all mental achievements is that criteria of success or failure can be ascribed to them.[9] There are ways of determining whether a person has or has not acquired a skill or understood a concept; exercise of intelligence presupposes the possibility of criticism and self-criticism. This is why the notion of heed is built into the notion of intelligent behaviour. The agent acts knowingly, on *qui vive*. He is not detached from his dispositions, motives, or emotions; they help to identify, for him and for others, what at any given moment he is. This includes moral dispositions as well. Ryle's views on moral philosophy are congruent with the ideas expressed in *The Concept of Mind*. In an early essay, written in 1940, 'Conscience and Moral Convictions', Ryle provided the following definition: 'Conscience, then, is one species, among others, of scrupulousness; and scrupulousness is the operative acceptance of a rule or principle which consists in the disposition to behave, in all modes of behaviour, including saying to oneself and others, teaching, chiding, etc., in accordance with the rule.'[10] In a paper written eighteen years later (almost ten years after the appearance of *The Concept of Mind*) and entitled 'On Forgetting the Difference Between Right and Wrong', Ryle explained why in his opinion it is ridiculous to say that one has forgotten the difference: 'To have been taught the difference is to have been brought to appreciate the difference, and this appreciation is not just a competence to label correctly or just a capacity to do things efficiently. It includes an inculcated caring, a habit of taking certain sorts of things seriously.'[11] Ryle added that 'a person who becomes less or more conscientious is a somewhat changed person.'

The inclusion of moral competences among the characteristics of the human mind underscores the distance between Ryle's position and Behaviourism. The very notion of competence, governed by criteria of success or failure corresponding to each type of competence, precludes the possibility of describing human actions in terms of witnessable behaviour alone. Human beings behave in terms of knowledge they acquired in the past which they keep incorporating into their responses in the light of given circumstances. In contrast to drill, training allows us to adjust our responses to the changing scene around us. 'Drill dispenses with intelligence, training develops it.'[12] To determine whether a performance is intelligent we must look beyond the performance itself and consider the powers and propensities which are exercised in performing the action.

One of the reasons why Ryle admired the novels of Jane Austen was that she depicted the human mind as exhibiting 'the whole complex unity of a conscious, thinking, feeling and acting person'. The copious and elastic discriminations among human capacities, already recognized by Aristotle, were expressed by Jane Austen in an ample, variegated and many-dimensional vocabulary. 'Her descriptions of people mention their tempers, habits, dispositions, moods, inclinations, impulses, sentiments, feelings, affections, thoughts, reflections, opinions, principles, prejudices, imaginations and fancies.'[13]

Conscious of the fact that in *The Concept of Mind* and in his other writings he had not given sufficient attention to one prominent display of mind, that of thinking in the sense of reflecting and pondering, Ryle devoted much attention to this topic in the later years of his life. On numerous occasions, both in the later stage and before, he called attention to the polymorphousness of the concept of thinking: 'Only some thinking is excogitation; only some thinking is work; only some thinking has a topic or a problem.'[14] Some thinking is just reverie or musing, intellectual doodling or strolling. There is another sort of distinction. When we ask what a person thinks, we may be inquiring about the opinions he holds or beliefs he entertains. This use of 'think' is to be distinguished from that in which the verb refers to actual activities of pondering, calculating, composing. Still another type of comparision is made when a Thinker is distinguished from an Agent and when the thinking is wholly theoretical and detached from the current practical tasks of the thinker.[15] These distinctions, and many others, Ryle discussed in some of the papers published in the second volume of his *Collected Papers*.[16] But he felt that they needed more attention and he proceeded to examine them in the papers comprising our collection, to which we now turn.

(1) 'Adverbial Verbs and Verbs of Thinking' explores a line of thought that goes back to some observations in *The Concept of Mind*[17] and has been already discussed by Ryle in some detail in 'Thinking and Reflecting'.[18] He did not conceal the fact that the ascription of adverbiality to some verbs of doing was only metaphorical. It was a deliberate device to steer us away from the Cartesian temptation to postulate an additional ghostly doing. Consider for example, a person who hurries over his breakfast. He is doing not two things, breakfasting and hurrying, but only one, namely, hurriedly breakfasting. This paraphrase explains why the metaphor of adverbiality seems appropriate. As Ryle also points out in this paper, the metaphor is not to be translated into 'acting in a certain manner' because

some qualifications of doings do not signify the style or procedure of the doing but rather its motive, as in 'venially', or its time reference, as in 'repeatedly'. By thinking 'adverbially' of some doings we will be looking beyond the performance to its surrounding characterizations which tell us something important about either the agent or the circumstances of the performance. When we learn that the soldier obeyed the sergeant's order, or that he performed the order reluctantly, we do learn something about his mind, without having to ascribe to him some invisible pushes or pulls.

Since adverbial ascriptions are not pointing to any separable doings, it would be a mistake, for instance, to look, with Wittgenstein, for some 'family resemblance' features in all instances of obeying or hurrying. Neither verb signifies an autonomous doing but derives its content from what Ryle in a later paper is going to call 'infra-doings' whose scope is too heterogeneous to encourage a hunt for common or even resemblance features.[19] The verb 'thinking' often functions adverbially; it characterizes some autonomous doings which could be performed unthinkingly. But when a person does something with his wits about him, heedfully, he can rightly be said to think what he is doing, although he is not performing any concomitant independent snatches of thinking.

Autonomous verbs of doing may have multiple layers of adverbialness attached to them. I may hurry over my breakfast obediently but also obey the order reluctantly, or, on top of that, pretend my reluctance. Again, when all four levels are applicable I am doing not four things – breakfasting, obeying, 'reluctating', and pretending – but only one. This ability to act from such pyramiding sophistication levels is also a characteristic of the human mind with which we are quite familiar and which may be seen more clearly if we look at it through the metaphor of adverbiality. Nevertheless, Ryle explicitly warns the reader: 'Obviously no weight can be put on to the back of this metaphor.' In fact, he suggests a variant to this metaphor by proposing that, in parallel to the nominalization of adjectives, for instance when we move from particular instances of 'wise' to 'wisdom', we may speak of ' "verb-izations" of de-particularized sentences and clauses in which adverbs and adverbial phrases more or less forcefully qualify their now de-particularized verbs'. Following such suggestions, we may break the hold of misleading pictures foisted on us by Cartesian epistemologies.

(2) In 'Thought and Soliloquy' Ryle defends the view that 'Some thinking does, but most thinking does not require the saying or sub-saying of anything'. Along the way he returns, with new examples, to his criticisms of the claim that thought must be *in* language or *in* symbols.[20] He also shows that there are many conceptual barnacles, largely ignored, in the idea of saying things to oneself. As usual, to make his point, he explores the neighbouring conceptual territory and resorts to some typically Rylean illustrations and turns of phrase: 'And I begin my inner sermon-recapitulation with "Dearly beloved brethren" and not with "Dearly beloved brother, Gilbert".'

Soliloquous activities may differ according to the purpose with which they are done, and each purpose has its own criteria of success. 'Meditating composingly and meditating self-practisingly are different things; their successes and failures are different, and can be interdependent.' Here we can make a connection with the previous discussion of the adverbiality of some verbs of doing, or with the possibility of discerning sophistication ladders of intention or of achievement. Not to be excluded is the possibility that some of our meditatings are conducted not with an ulterior *supra*-motive but done simply for their own sake. (In this context Ryle parenthetically makes an interesting historical comment. It struck him as curious that the very special instances of mental doodling or visualizing have been taken by epistemologists like Hume 'as the primary or original sort of thinking'.)

Among the possible 'adverbial' characterizations of inner soliloquy or pondering may be included a heuristic purpose. It is often true of a thinker that he does not yet know *what* to think – this is why he is thinking. That heuristic character of the activity of thinking will of course constitue, at least for the time being, the top of the pyramid or sophistication ladder, with all other '*infra*-doings' forming the relevant background. Here one may include not only such highly theoretical levels of inquiry as those of a Euclid or a Kant, but also an exercise of a schoolboy attempting to arrive at the correct solution of a difficult multiplication problem.

An alternative to describing some activities as involving several rungs of a sophistication ladder would be to say that some activities are parasitic on others. Even the phrase 'thinking about thinking' can be understood only if we acknowledge the presence of two levels. The 'host-parasite' metaphor is to be taken as value-neutral and merely calling attention to the presence of the two levels of one activity, and one should not be tempted to separate them, in Cartesian fashion, into two independent activities.

(3) Since most of the papers in our collection were intended for oral delivery, their content is not so closely packed as are some other of Ryle's writings, and they abound in helpful illustrations. This is particularly true of 'Thought and Imagination'. Ryle's contrast between the styles of the two imaginary historians is drawn effectively and engagingly. The topic of imagination was of interest to him throughout his philosophical career. Long before writing the chapter on Imagination in *The Concept of Mind* he had presented, in 1933, a paper, 'Imaginary Objects', before the Aristotelian Society. Nor was he uncritical of his own views.[21] In the paper included in this collection he distinguishes among three ways in which the relation between imagination and thought may be conceived, and his main conclusion is that there is an exercise of imagination which is not a rival or supplanter of thinking, but rather, to fall back on Ryle's previously coined metaphor, 'adverbially' qualifies thinking. Ryle hoped that his discussion of thought and imagination would diminish our persistent temptation to *contrast* them. There are of course intellectual tasks in which the exercise of imagination is uncalled for or undesirable, for example, in producing correct answers in arithmetic. Similarly, the subject matter to which imagination is applied imposes constraining conditions of its own; a historian must not allow his imagination to distort or ignore facts. But there are tasks in which hard factual thinking and imaginative thinking go hand in hand. The inventions of an Edison or theoretical discoveries of a Faraday are a result of a successful blend of the two forms of mental powers.

One and the same piece of information may become or fail to become a stepping-stone to further imaginative uses of that information. Many a thinker proceeds along uncharted paths, and often this kind of thinking leads to new or useful or important knowledge. In other instances the result may be an impressive innovative work of art – a poem, a novel, a sculpture, a symphony. Each type of achievement has its own standards of excellence and failure, and it is by reference to such standards that the complex collaboration of imagination and thought can be judged. Although Ryle's allusions to historiography or art are almost casual, they are stimulating enough to be of interest to philosophers of history or aestheticians. Also, it is not untypical of him to wind up his serious enquiry with a teasing joke.

(4) The title of the next paper, 'Thinking and Self-Teaching', gives away its philosophical point. Ryle directs our attention to another interesting connection of the concept of thinking to other concepts, this time to teaching. The connection is not usually made, but by the time Ryle has explained it, it appears intriguing and impressive. The paper starts with some comments on teaching itself and could be read with profit by students in schools of education. But the weight of Ryle's argument falls on the close parallel between thinking and self-teaching. The ingenious twist given to the famous example from the *Meno* is of value not only because it tickles our imagination but also, and primarily, because it so effectively makes Ryle's point. The illustration reaches, critically, deep into the recesses of Platonic metaphysics, for it questions the meaningfulness of Plato's claim that souls could acquire knowledge directly from the forms. Ryle's argument is that the variegated steps and dodges which Socrates takes in reawakening in the slave boy some 'forgotten' geometrical truths are exactly the same steps that Socrates himself could take to think out these truths, should he have forgotten them. The procedures in coming to know something may be exactly the same, and we could just as well call them 'self-teaching' as 'thinking'.[22] Or, to put it in Ryle's own concluding words: 'Thinking is trying to better one's own instructions, it is to try out promissory tracks which will exist, if they ever do exist, only after one has stumbled exploringly over ground where they are not.'

(5) 'Thinking and Saying' returns to some of the ground covered previously, but with a difference. Again Ryle reviews his motivating reasons for re-exploring this philosophical territory, and he introduces a new pair of labels to dub the two positions from which his own diverges. This time he contrasts it with the 'Deflationary' and the 'Inflationary' tempers, the slogan of the first being 'Nothing But . . .', and 'Something Else As Well . . .' that of the second. Untypically perhaps, the paper contains many names of philosophers, modern and contemporary, whom Ryle deems guilty of subjecting the phenomena of mind to 'categorical maltreatments'. But these are helpful historical reminders, enabling us to see just what bothered Ryle about the received theories of knowledge. He finds a new name for the duplicationist epistemology insistent on introducing special hidden entities *in* which or *in terms of* which we supposedly think; he calls the position the 'vehicle-cargo' model and recommends that we begin by jettisoning it.[23] Words, for Ryle, are institutional *enabling*-instruments and can be employed for multiple purposes in writing, in speech, in heuristic soliloquizing. If we ask what the latter use consists in, there is no one-strand answer. One important use is experimental, exploratory, describable as path-finding and not as path-following. What we should try to determine is the governing purposes of a piece of thinking, and that will tell us in what specific way the powers of the mind are being used, without licensing us to invent generic slogans.

(6) Although 'Mowgli in Babel' was published a few months after 'Negative "Actions" ', the closeness of its content to that of the preceding paper justifies a slight departure from our chronological sequence. One of the reasons for placing it next is that it too has a historical interest. Written as a review of Zeno Vendler's *Res Cogitans*, it shows us how Ryle viewed some of the philosophical doctrines current in his time. He endorsed in Vendler's and Chomsky's versions of Neo-Cartesianism some effective and powerful ways of showing the absurdities of behaviourist reductionism, but he was in deep disagreement with them when they proceeded from 'Nothing But . . .' to 'Something Else As Well . . .'. Neither a Platonic Two nor a Quinean One is the correct answer to the question about the

nature of thinking. In Vendler's case Ryle pointed to the arbitrary choice of some verbs of thinking to defend the doctrine of 'the almost universal identity of the objects of speech and thought' and adduced the whole plethora of verbs of thinking that fail to fit Vendler's model. Ryle heartily endorsed Vendler's rejection of any theory that defines knowledge in terms of belief. But he attacked with considerable vehemence the Chomsky/Vendler theory that learning to speak (and think, for that matter) presupposes the ability to decode some deep syntax structure (Chomsky) or some innate vocabulary-items (Vendler).[24]

(7) What Ryle discusses in his 'Negative "Actions"' paper seems truly a new discovery.[25] It throws further light on the appearance of elusiveness in some phenomena of thinking. By lifting out for our attention a collection of verbs that do not seem to be verbs of doing at all and yet are needed to fully characterize the agent's involvement in a given state of affairs, Ryle has added more fuel to his contention that a correct account of thinking does not require a postulation of some secret occult goings on in disembodied recesses of the mind.[26]

The verbs in question refer to the agent's intentional non-performance of some specifiable actions: refraining, postponing, overlooking, letting, pausing – to mention but a few from a longer string Ryle provides. Although in some cases there seem to be some reasons to regard such verbs as verbs of doing, the preponderance of reasons is against regarding them as such. And yet their role in describing some behaviour is indispensable. In what terms can we characterize them? Since on the basis of views developed in *The Concept of Mind* one might be inclined to dub Ryle's view of mind as dispositional, one might also ask whether the verbs we are examining connote dispositions. Ryle considers this possibility but rejects it. Nor does he think that the resort to 'consciousness' will help to account for these verbs. Once more, he finds the notion 'of a higher order' illuminating. Negative 'actions' provide the *supra*-factor (postponing) ascribable to *infra*-doings (writing a letter). The logical problem of reference in case the letter never gets written is solved by recognizing that the connection of the verb is not to the non-existent act, but only to the act-description, and Ryle finds here an interesting parallel to the operation of negation as such. While not actions proper, negative 'actions' are intentional sustained actualities, truly or falsely predictable of agents. They may be used to identify 'lines of action' which agents at any given time may be correctly said to pursue. The acknowledgement of the presence of negative 'actions' in our behaviour enlarges our concept of the 'mental' without forcing us into a Cartesian position. But as Ryle concludes, some Cartesian genies may be both relieved and released.

(8) The final paper, 'Improvisation', echoes some of the findings established while discussing the role of imagination. Ryle gives reasons why he prefers the term 'improvisation' to 'imagination', 'originality', and 'creativity' (the latter term being particularly repellent to him). By now we should not be surprised to find Ryle pointing to the importance of innovation, experimentation, improvisation. He had been doing so all along, beginning with the early statements in *The Concept of Mind*, where he contrasted drill and training, the latter always requiring some degree of alertness to the unroutine elements in our experience. In this paper that element is recognized as *logically* necessary. 'To a partly novel situation the response is necessarily partly novel, else it is not a response.' Ryle claims that innovative thinking is not absent even from inferring itself. Between some premises and some conclusions there are no intermediate steps, and only inference-trained minds are presupposed. In some situations we can find the long-eluded solution from the data and premises that were always available to us, and we can do so not because some additional intermediary steps have turned up, thus changing our question, but simply because *we* have changed and can now see, with new eyes, so to speak, what we previously failed to see. The penultimate paragraph of the paper contains a sentence which could be regarded as a summary of Ryle's labours in the conceptual vineyards of thinking. 'So thinking, I now declare quite generally is, at the least, the engaging of partly trained wits in a partly fresh situation.'

K. KOLENDA

RICE UNIVERSITY,
HOUSTON, TEXAS

NOTES

1 Cf. Ryle's autobiographical remarks in *Ryle*, A Collection of Critical Essays, O. P. Wood and G. Pitcher, eds. (New York: Doubleday), 1970, pp. 6–10. Also consider his response in *A Symposium on Gilbert Ryle, Rice University Studies*, Vol. 58, Nr. 3, 1972, pp. 108–9: 'Kolenda slides rather casually past the Russellian notion of the nonsensical versus the true-or-false; and past Wittgenstein's derivative and diversified notion of what is and what is not in breach of "logical grammar". But for some of us these notions not only affected the procedures of our thinking; they were also constant and central topics of our thought. I hope that we were, quite often, conceptual Philanthropists; but we were also, very often, aspiring philosophical technicians.'

2 *Dilemmas* (Cambridge University Press), 1956, p. 7.

3 Cf., for instance, Ryle's characterization of philosophical notions as 'inter-departmental' in 'Abstractions', *Collected Papers* (hereafter referred to as *CP*), Vol. 2, p. 440 (London: Hutchinson), 1971.

4 *CP*, Vol. 2, p. viii.

5 On one occasion, while discussing with Tony Palmer and me the just published 'Negative "Actions" ', he expressed the opinion that he was pretty close to getting the issues straight, but even then he felt that more needed to be done on the topic.

6 *The Concept of Mind* (hereafter referred to as *CM*) (Harmondsworth: Penguin), 1963, p. 45.

7 *CM*, p. 283.

8 *Ibid.*, p. 284.

9 *CM*, pp. 40 ff. See also 'John Locke' in *CP*, Vol. 1, pp. 153–54.

10 *CP*, Vol. 2, p. 191.

11 *CP*, Vol. 2, pp. 387–88. See also 'Rational Animal' in *CP*, Vol. 2. 'The thinker cares, at least a little bit, whether he gets things right or wrong; he is at least slightly concerned to think properly.' (p. 432).

12 *CM*, p. 42.

13 'Jane Austen and the Moralists', *CP*, Vol. 1, p. 289. See also a fuller, typically Rylean characterization of human nature in 'Rational Animal', *CP*, Vol. 2, p. 417.

14 'Thinking and Language', *CP*, Vol. 2, p. 258. In a paper entitled 'Polymorphous Concepts' and published in *Ryle* (*op. cit.*), J. O. Urmson finds some unclarities in the way Ryle characterizes polymorphous concepts, such as *thinking* and *working*. He also claims that, for Ryle's purposes, his formal account is too wide.

15 'Rational Animal', *CP*, Vol. 2, p. 422.

16 There is an extensive critical discussion of these papers by F. N. Sibley in an article entitled 'Ryle and Thinking' in *Ryle, op. cit.*

17 '. . . it is quite idiomatic to replace the heed verb by a heed adverb.' *CM*, p. 232.

18 *CP*, Vol. 2, pp. 465–479.

19 The heterogeneity of 'thinking' is evident in Ryle's list in 'Thinking', *CP*, Vol. 2, p. 297. The concluding comment is worth noting: 'To look for some common and peculiar ingredients of all thinking is like looking for an ingredient common and peculiar to cat's-cradle, hide-and-seek, billiards, snap and all the other things we call "games".'

20 Cf. 'Thinking and Language', *CP*, Vol. 2, pp. 262 ff.

21 'Phenomenology Versus "The Concept of Mind",' *CP*, Vol. 1, p. 194.

22 Cf. *CM*, p. 142. Also 'John Locke', *CP*, Vol. 1, p. 155.

23 It is of interest to note that on this question Ryle's views changed considerably over the years. Cf., for example, 'Are There Propositions?' (*CP*, Vol. 2, p. 31), where Ryle said that 'if I am thinking I must be thinking *in* and *in terms of* something. I refer of course to thinking *in* images or *in* words.'

24 The vigour with which Ryle rejected the current versions of Neo-Cartesianism, and his eloquent defence of a theory of learning based on views developed in *The Concept of Mind* and later essays, betray something that he was reluctant to attribute to himself, namely, that his philosophy was motivated by the desire to restore a more balanced picture of the human mind. The title of my contribution to our *Symposium on Gilbert Ryle* (*op. cit.*) was 'The Recovery of the Human' and intended to point up the positive results stemming from the rejection of Reductionism and Duplicationism. But Ryle was anxious to dispel the impression that in his major work he 'was engaged in a task of heroic knight-errantry on behalf of the oppressed concept of Man'. (p. 108). It did not feel like that to him at the time, he protested. Like most of his colleagues, he was intent on clearing up some specific philosophical muddles. There was an interesting sequel to this exchange, however. Impressed by the vigour with which Ryle exposed Vendler's errors in the review, I had written to Ryle, indicating that in my symposium paper I wanted to call attention to the underlying concern on his part that we do subscribe to defensible views about the mind. At least, the review betrayed a strong presence of this concern. To which Ryle replied in a letter: 'I grant you that, and 25% of the other', referring, of course, to the characterization of his views in my 'Recovery of the Human'. These points are worth making if one is of the opinion, as I am, that Ryle's concern about our intellectual health is important and that his writings contributed a lot toward restoring such health, if not by direct intention, then at least through actual results of his work. (In this

connection, Ryle's view of Wittgenstein's way of philosophizing (see Appendix) is of considerable interest.)

25 There are some tentative forerunners in Ryle's earlier work, however. Cf. *CM*, p. 255: '. . . the operations consist of *abstentions* from producing them.' (Italics added).

26 Tony Palmer has called my attention to one advantage the negative-'actions' account has over Ryle's previous characterizations: it permits the 'pyramiding effect' without requiring some neutral doings as their foundation.

1

Adverbial Verbs and Verbs of Thinking

My long-range objective is to find out how to talk sense about the thinking that *Le Penseur* is occupied in doing without committing (1) the Category-howler of Behaviourism or (2) the Category-howler of Cartesianism – that is, (1) without trying to *Reduce* thinking to what it isn't, for example, to audible soliloquizing; and (2) without trying to evaluate it by *Duplicating* it with some bits of inaudible because 'mental' soliloquizing.

It is for the sake of this long-range objective and not just for its own sake that I want to begin by drawing your attention to a special class of verbs, which I prefatorily and metaphorically label 'Adverbial Verbs'. Much, very much later on, I shall suggest that we should non-metaphorically label them 'Abstract Verbs' on the analogy of 'Abstract Nouns'. Here is a batch of my Adverbial Verbs: hurry, hesitate, persevere, obey, disobey, take care, attend, rehearse, play, pretend, enjoy, accelerate, cooperate, experiment, succeed, fail, abstain, bungle, recur, shirk. The common feature for which I select them is this: there is and can be no such thing as, for example, just obeying *per se* or just accelerating *per se*. Something positive or concrete must be being done for taking care, rehearsing or cooperating to be being done. I can slope arms obediently or disobediently; I can stand still obediently or disobediently, but I cannot just be obeying or disobeying *sans phrase*. I obey the order to slope arms just by sloping arms; I cannot obey the order by doing something else or by doing nothing instead. Whether breakfasting or lecturing I can do so hurriedly or in a hurry; but if, without any such underlying positive or *per se* action being mentioned or understood, you just order me to hurry, then there is nothing, however vague, disjunctive or equivocal, that you have told or forbidden me to do, nothing, my doing or not doing which qualifies as doing something that you ordered or forbade. In

17

reported how I was occupied at midday, you cannot say that I
was occupied just in shirking, bungling, perservering, failing,
attempting, practising, shamming or repeating. 'Obey!' *is* not the
command that I am to obey, nor *is* 'Please' the request with which
I do or do not comply.

If I obeyed, I did *something* concrete that I had been ordered to
do; but saying just that I obeyed does not specify what this
concrete something was that I did and was ordered to do. Let us
stay for a minute or two with this familiar notion of obeying.

The soldier, ordered by the Sergeant Major to slope arms,
obeys just by sloping arms. But he might, when showing off to
his fiancée, slope arms without being ordered. We ask the
Behaviourist, 'What is the difference between sloping arms in
obedience to an order and just sloping arms?' The Behaviourist
peers and listens, and finds no behavioural difference, so he
plays the Reductionist trick. He says, 'Obeying the order to
slope arms is *Nothing But* sloping arms. There isn't something
else that the soldier does *as well*.' So there is no such thing as
obeying or disobeying – which is rubbish. The Cartesian
rightly rejects this Reductionist trick, and says, 'Obeying the
order to slope arms does not *reduce* to just sloping arms; so the
soldier both slopes arms (and we witness him doing this) and
also does Something Else as Well that we do not witness,
namely in his consciousness – and what he does in that
shadowy cabinet is a non-muscular and noiseless act of, so to
speak, mentally sloping a mental rifle on to a mental shoulder.'
Yet our Cartesian has to allow that the Sergeant Major has not
ordered this second mental action, so it is not by performing this
postulated second, internal action that the soldier does what the
Sergeant ordered. The Sergeant knows whether his order to
slope arms has been obeyed or disobeyed, without trying to pry
into the soldier's consciousness. How then are we to achieve a
non-Reductionist and also non-Duplicationist account of
obeying? My long-range problem is a generalization of this in
itself tiny question.

It is a frequent though not universal feature of these Adverbial
Verbs that, in English at least, significant sentences
incorporating them can generally be paraphrased by sentences
containing some adverb or adverbial phrase instead. If I was
taking care or decelerating, then I was doing something
concrete, for example *driving*, carefully or doing something

concrete, for instance *singing*, more and more slowly. But this clue must not be trusted very far. If I am driving and taking care, there is only one thing that I must be doing, namely driving. But I may be driving and singing, and so doing two independent positive or *per se* things, either of which I could continue to do after ceasing to do the other. But I could still be described adverbially as driving with a song and perhaps more disputably as driving songfully. What is much more important is this: adverbial verbs, and their corresponding adverbs, if any, can very often, if not always, be paraphrased by simple or complex subordinate clauses. 'Tommy obeyed the order to slope arms' = (roughly) 'Tommy sloped arms immediately after he heard the command to do so and *because* he heard and recognized that command'. Aristotle would draw attention to the fact that adverbial verbs can have opposites, like 'hurry-dawdle', 'obey-disobey', 'continue-cease'. Verbs of *per se* doing apparently cannot.

One or two other incidental points.

(1) I stupidly got the idea at school that as adjectives signify qualities (which is sometimes true but often false), so adverbs qualifying verbs, for example verbs of doing or happening, characterize what is being done or happening as being done or happening *in a certain manner* or *in a certain way*. This too is sometimes true but often false. 'Dexterously', 'awkwardly' and '*sotto voce*' accept the description pretty well; 'unexpectedly', 'visibly', 'unprecedentedly', 'luckily', 'repeatedly', 'obediently', 'venially', 'venally', 'illegally' and 'inadvertently' not at all. The adverb 'maliciously' signifies the motive of an action, not its style or procedure. The adverb 'recently' signifies the rough, relative date of an action or happening, not its manner. And so on.

(2) A great many fully fledged positive verbs of doing already carry with them the force of some specific adverb. Incorrectness is already connoted by 'misspell', so that 'misspell incorrectly' is a redundancy and 'misspell correctly' is already ruled out. So are 'scrutinize inattentively', 'bargain unintentionally', 'murder ineffectually' and 'damage innocuously'. I hope in the end to show that verbs of reflecting, deliberating, calculating and so on, are of this class, though in a special corner of this class.

As 'hurry' and 'obey' are active verbs, there exists a temptation, stemming from an erroneous grammatical presupposition, that they are therefore verbs of doing. So as I can obey by, or hurry over, my breakfasting and my preaching, my multiplying or my resigning, and as these are in other ways hugely disparate doings, we are tempted to search for some latent and generic action-kind that is common to all of them, to render them all as species, however disparate, of the postulated generic activities of obeying or hurrying – for all that other breakfastings, preachings, multiplyings and resignings, being as spontaneous or sluggish as you please, are not specimens of obeying or hurrying. We may then fall for Wittgenstein's notion of family-likeness-concepts, and try to find respects in which, say, the breakfaster's hurrying or obeying is a bit like the preacher's, and this a bit like the multiplier's and this a bit like the resigner's, though breakfasting is not a bit like resigning. But this is unnecessary. The verbs 'obey' and 'hurry' are not verbs of doing, not even highly generic, elastic, clannish or latitudinarian verbs of doing. There is nothing, however vaguely or multiply disjunctive, that you have told or asked or advised me to do, when you have shouted 'Obey' (period), 'Repeat' (period), or 'Hurry' (period). You have not given an accommodating or latitudinarian order or request; you just have not finished giving an order or request. Wittgenstein's own favoured example of game-playing (though he unfortunately stressed the noun rather than the verb) seems to me a clear case of an adverbial verb being misdiagnosed as itself a highly hospitable verb of doing. The report that during a certain period John was playing is not, as Wittgenstein seems to have thought, just vague, unspecific, elastic or disjunctive; it is unfinished. For it to be true or false there must have been a positive, concrete or *per se* something that he was doing with a name and a description of its own, like wheeling a wheelbarrow or hitting a ball. Whatever it is that he was doing, he might have been doing just that, but not playing, just as whatever is being done hurriedly or obediently or for the second time, just that might have been being done unhurriedly and spontaneously or disobediently and for the first or the eleventh time.

I am now going to coin for you three new verbs which non-archaic English lacks, though Latin has them, namely the verbs to 'reluctate', 'obstinate' and 'vigilate', corresponding to our familiar adverbs 'reluctantly', 'obstinately' and 'vigilantly'. With these verbs we can now assert or deny that, or question whether someone was at a certain time reluctating, obstinating or vigilating. You, piously believing that active verbs *ipso facto* signify actions or activities, now set to work to identify the genera or species that include all cases and only cases of reluctating, obstinating and vigilating, but to your dismay you find that things as different as bird-watching, awaiting the train, and marking an examination-paper can all alike be, but can also all alike *not* be, done reluctantly, obstinately and vigilantly. What then *is* a person engaged in who is obstinating? and what is he *not* engaged in who is obstinating? And can he reluctate reluctantly – or non-reluctantly? Are there, even, any sorts at all of doings which are not sometimes sorts or varieties of obstinating, though sometimes sorts or varieties of non-obstinating? How multifarious and how patchy or thinly spread can family-likenesses between these postulated actions become, before the action-family itself evaporates into thin air? It is not that, as Wittgenstein would seemingly have thought, that the command 'Reluctate' (period) can be obeyed in a great many equally good alternative, though more or less unresembling ways, but that it cannot be obeyed or disobeyed at all. It is not a *liberal*, but an *unfinished* command.

Here the advertised manufacturedness of my new active verbs 'reluctate', 'obstinate' and 'vigilate' gives the game away from the start. Of course these are not verbs of doing, so the question: What general or special sorts of doings do they and do they not signify? has no answer. We have never even wanted the verbs, in order to be able to report what someone is doing. We had already all the verbs of doing that we needed. We also had the adverbs that we needed, including 'reluctantly', 'obstinately' and 'vigilantly'. That is why you were not even minimally grateful for my additions to your stock of active verbs. They did not enable or help you to enjoin, forbid or report any actions that you could not enjoin, forbid or report without them.

Before going ahead to apply to philosophically interesting matters this notion of metaphorical Adverbialness, I want just to mention some active verbs which not being verbs of doing, also require the backing of proper verbs of *per se* doing, though not quite in any of the same ways as those I have so far cited. The active verbs 'stop', 'start' and 'continue' are such. If I order you to stop, start or continue, there must be some ulterior *per se* X-ing, explicitly or implicitly specified, if my order is to have an obeyable or disobeyable content. You must be, or be potentially about to be, doing something, like typing, holding your breath or gazing at something, for you to be able to stop doing *it*, to go on doing *it* or to start doing *it*. The exasperated teacher who tells the children to stop doing *whatever* they are doing, can be obeyed by their ceasing to do all sorts of different things. But for each child, who is in a position to obey, there must be at least one X-ing which he is doing and can therefore stop doing, no matter how unlike it may be to what his neighbour is doing. Perhaps one obediently stops breathing while the other obediently stops holding his breath. What cannot be the case, though, is that Sally should obey by stopping stopping (period) or that Tommy should obey by stopping starting (period) or stopping continuing (period).

I now turn to applications. Take the two different but related notions of trying and intending. Philosophers have sometimes found both *trying* and *intending* elusive notions. I suspect that their embarrassment has sometimes been due to their presupposition that 'try' and 'intend', being active verbs, ought to signify *per se* doings – *per se* doings, indeed, of auxiliary or back-stage sorts, but still doings specifically and numerically different from the doings to which they are auxiliary or backstage. So they have hankered to say that the sedulous whistler is doing two separately do-able things, namely whistling and trying, or maybe three separately do-able things, namely whistling and trying and intending. On such a view whistling intentionally would differ from whistling absent-mindedly in the same sort of way as driving with a song differs from driving without a song – save that singing is mere concomitant of driving, whereas intending to whistle is sup-posedly not just a fortuitous concomitant, but an auxiliary one, to some whistling. To any such interpretation of these active verbs the right reply is that 'he was trying . . .', and 'he was meaning to . . .' are unfinished reports. The verbs are auxiliary verbs, but they do not signify auxiliary actions, since they do not in any way signify actions – or, of course, inactions, like waiting – or passions, like fretting, either. A person trying for a bet to sing 'Home, Sweet Home' in under four minutes, is tackling one task, not two or three tasks. That he has not succeeded yet is part of what 'he is trying to . . .' signifies; and this is not another thing that he is doing. That he is doing it not absent-mindedly but on purpose; and that he is not, by mistake, singing, say, 'Rule Britannia' in lieu of 'Home Sweet Home' are part of what is signified by 'he is doing it intentionally', and these too are not extra things that he is doing or might be ordered or requested to do by themselves.

I can now come to the near-centre of my target. If a person is taking care, he is X-ing more or less carefully, that is not totally carelessly. In his X-ing – it may be his typing or tree-climbing – he is either avoiding known mistakes and inefficiencies or he is repairing those that he has committed, and avoiding committing them again. He is applying in his present undertaking some already learned precautions and corrections. If you like, his present activity is 'rule-governed' in that 'rules' previously learned by instruction or by personal trial and error are now strongly or weakly controlling his movements. But I prefer to say, less stuffily, that a person's trying to type or climb involves his trying to get things correct, unawkward or un-chancey for example, already knowing at least some faults for faults and some risks for risks. In his typing or climbing he has his wits about him, unlike the man in a panic or a daze, and his wits are at least partly trained or practised wits, unlike those of the absolute novice. For however excellent may be the native or unschooled wits of the absolute novice, he cannot avoid, lament or correct mistypings or misspellings, since he has not begun to learn how to type or how to spell. He cannot even make mistakes. Infants in the cradle commit no fallacies, no misspellings, no miscalculations – and no social gaffes either. Now if someone is doing something on purpose and exercising some ordinary care in doing it; and if, moreover, he is learning something, or at least being ready to learn something, however minimal, from his successes, failures, difficulties and facilities, so that he is in fact, if not in intention, tending to improve as he goes along, we shall not and should not hesitate to say that he is thinking what he is doing. He himself deplores some of his lapses, omissions, falterings and inadequacies in epistemic terms of abuse as mistakes, misestimates, muddles or at least stupidities.

If I am right, then here we have one notion of thinking, though not the only one – and it is an adverbial notion, indeed, a multiply adverbial notion. It would be an unfinished report, to say of the typist or the climber just that he was thinking (period) or experimenting (period) or persevering (period) or taking care (period). He was typing or climbing with his partially trained and practised wits about him; but he was exercising those wits in his typing or climbing, and not in doing something else concomitant with, or even auxiliary to his typing or climbing. Or if he did now and then pause to reflect about Gödel's theorem, or even about his typing or climbing, it was not for these collateral reflectings that we describe him as typing or climbing carefully or with his wits about him. If at certain moments he had let his attention wander from his typing or climbing to some theoretical problem about Gödel or to some methodological problem about this typing or climbing, then so far from thinking what he was doing, he was, during these moments, *not* thinking what he was doing. He was, during those moments, typing or climbing, absentmindedly or mechanically, and therefore without any care. Such collateral reflections would be rivals to his minding his typing or climbing business, and might even be detrimental to it. (The Centipede . . .)

To X, thinking what one is doing, is not to be doing both some X-ing and some separately do-able Y-ing; it is to be X-ing under a variety of qualifications, such as X-ing on purpose, with some tentativeness, some vigilance against some known hazards, some perseverance and with at least a modicum of intended or unintended self-training. It is to X intentionally, experimentally, circumspectly and practisingly, and these by themselves are not additional things that he is doing or might be doing.

Two grumbles always come up at this point. Grumble A is that I have said nothing about what *Le Penseur* is engaged in, that is about the person who is engaged in the thinking of thoughts. He is surely so meditating, reflecting, pondering or thinking that the report 'he is thinking' is *not* an unfinished, adverbial report. This grumble is fully justified. The notion of thinking what one is doing does not amount to any of the notions of for example meditating, reflecting, examining, deliberating, pondering, or calculating. The telephone interrupts the typist's attentive and careful typing; but it interrupts *Le Penseur*'s attentive and careful thinking. I hope that the notion of thinking what one is doing provides letters of the alphabet out of which we shall be able to spell what *Le Penseur* is engaged in. But it does not provide much of that spelling.

Grumble B is that if the typist is thinking what she is doing, then she *must* be doing little snatches of what *Le Penseur* does long stretches of. To be X-ing purposively, experimentally, cautiously, systematically and self-coachingly *must* be not only to be X-ing but also to be Y-ing, and therefore Pensant. However alert and assiduous the typist or the climber may be in their typing or climbing, they cannot be exercising their partly trained wits just by typing neatly and accurately or just by climbing unhazardously and efficiently, but only by collaterally being butterfly-like *Penseurs*, that is by collaterally doing some fleeting, separately-do-able cicumspectings and purposings.

This second grumble, so far from being justified, is, in a very important way, 180 per cent wrong-headed. It makes the alphabet a by-product of spelling. For *Le Penseur* himself cannot in logic be absent-mindedly, mechanically or vacantly or frantically meditating, analysing, calculating, examining, revising, composing or deliberating. Like the typist he must be doing whatever he is doing on purpose, and, in some degree, tentatively, circumspectly, unrecklessly, perseveringly and practisingly, in a word, with his wits about him. Otherwise he is not pondering – namely, not trying to solve his problem or complete his undertaking. In the thinking of thoughts, no less than in typing or composing music, the agent must be thinking what he is doing and this thinking what he is doing cannot be carved off into a second, collateral thinking of thoughts, even of self-didactic admonishing thoughts – otherwise *Le Penseur* could never get started. He could never tackle a problem on purpose or circumspectly, if his purposings and circumspectings had themselves to be extra purposive and circumspect doings.

It follows that *Le Penseur* cannot be, for example, trying to solve an abstract problem, unless there is some positive, concrete, or *per se* thing that he is doing, purposively, experimentally, carefully and perseveringly, such that he might have been doing just that positive or concrete thing absent-mindedly or mechanically. But just what is this positive or concrete thing? Breakfasting is a positive thing that a man may be hurrying over, but might do unhurriedly; sloping arms is a concrete thing that a soldier may do obediently, but might do spontaneously, disobediently, mechanically or just vacantly. But what is *Le Penseur* doing with his wits about him that he might have done when vacant, frantic, dazed, sleepwalking or when concentrating on some extraneous matter, like a football match? Here we have the adverbial verbs that we need, but we seem to be at a loss for the desiderated non-adverbial or autonomous verbs.

Part of our bafflement is relieved when we remind ourselves that there need not be just a single candidate for the vacancy, but a crowd of eligible candidates. For example, if *Le Penseur* is trying to compose a melody, then he is very likely to be humming notes and sequences of notes, aloud, under his breath or in his head – not just humming them, of course, but humming them experimentally, suspiciously, cancellingly, rehearsingly, recapitulatingly, and so on. These very notes and note sequences that he hums composingly, he might, by chance, have hummed gramophonically and with his mind on something else. Or if *Le Penseur* is trying to render an English poem into French, while he is unlikely to be humming notes and note-sequences, he is likely instead to be murmuring under his breath or in his head, French words and phrases, murmuring them, of course, experimentally, suspiciously, cancellingly, rehearsingly, recapitulatingly; and, again, any one or even all of these very same French words and phrases might have been muttered by him in delirium or by rote. Or he might be trying to find out how many letters there are in the Greek alphabet, in which case he is likely to be muttering *sotto voce* or in his head the sequence of Greek letter-names *'alpha'*, *'beta'*, *'gamma'*, etc. in meticulous parallel with the sequence of number-words 'one', 'two', 'three', etc. He too, or his parrot, might, perhaps by rote, have muttered 'alpha, one, beta, two, gamma, three . . .' and so on when he was not trying to find out how many letters there are in the Greek alphabet. If he were doing any of these things, or with his partly trained wits about him, minding what he was doing, he would, I think, qualify as reflecting or meditating, though of course we hope that *Le Penseur*'s task is a grander one than those of translating or counting. But if he does so qualify, then we do have here some satisfactory candidates for the vacancy that I postulated. There really are, in these cases, some positive, concrete, *per se,* non-adverbial, things that *Le Penseur* is doing, perhaps even audibly doing, in composing, translating and counting, which are such that he might have audibly done these self-same things non-translatingly and nonenumeratingly, that is, as Behaviourists would relish them. They are considerably different from one another, and this very fact of their differences already dispels our original expectation – which has been the expectation of too many psychologists and epistemologists – that there must exist some one, homogeneous X-ing such that for a person to be reflecting or meditating he must be X-ing.

I expect that you would like me here to go on to apply what I have just said to the grander thinkings that we hope *Le Penseur* is engaged in. For if he is, as he may be, a Newton or a Kant, a Dante or a Gödel, a Savonarola or a Bismarck, then he is likely to be doing something different not merely in degree but in level of sophistication from what my counter of letters or translator is doing. Unlike theirs, his thinking may merit a capital 'T', and, very likely, be far above our heads. Well I am going to disappoint this expectation, save for dropping one hint, which I have not myself been able to follow up more than an inch or two.

To have learned to recite correctly and readily the numbers 'one' 'two' 'three', etc. is not yet to have learned to count things such as raindrops on the window-pane. Miscounting these is not a case of getting the number-series wrong. Next, having learned how to count things is not yet to have learned how to reckon, for example to add or multiply. A mis-multiplication is not a mis-count. The success/failure conditions of multiplying require a higher level of sophistication than those of counting, as those of counting require a higher level of sophistication than those of reeling off the numbers one, two, three, or Eeny, Meeny. . . .

Multiplying *and* mis-multiplying presuppose counting, and counting *and* miscounting presuppose knowing one's numbers. So what number-words contribute to the thinking of the reckoner is different, in level, not just in degree, of accomplishment, from what they contribute to the thinking of the counter, and this, in its turn, differs, not in degree but in level of accomplishment, from what they contribute to the thinking of the child non-mechanically reciting his numbers. (I could have used instead the sophistication-levels or learning layers of alphabet-reciting, spelling and writing prose.)

These are diminutive and familiar sophistication-ladders or accomplishment-ladders. I guess that the description of

capital lettered Thinking would require the tracing of
very long, many-runged, sophistication-ladders – ladders the
bottom-rungs of which would still be such concrete, *per se*,
doings as hummings, word-utterings, etc., that is concrete or
per se doings which could be mechanical *or* purposive,
absent-minded *or* careful, and so on. Now with this topless
pyramiding of accomplishment-levels there will go a topless
pyramiding of adverbial verbs – and this we can easily
illustrate for ourselves. Repeating an action is doing it again, and
obediently repeating it is doing it again in obedience to an order.
Someone might be reluctantly obeying an order to do it again, or
even be repentently reluctant to obey the order to repeat what
he had said or done.

Let me here interpolate a minor safeguarding remark. So far I
have been treating *Le Penseur* as a man who is trying to
solve a problem, or perhaps a battery of problems. But this
could be over-restrictive. Not all pondering or musing is
problem-tackling. While some walking is exploring and some
walking is trying to get to a destination, still some walking is
merely taking a walk, and some walking is merely strolling
around. Similarly while some meditating or ruminating is
exploratory, and some, like multiplying, is travelling on
business, still some is just re-visiting familiar country and some
is just cogitative strolling for cogitative strolling's sake. Even *Le
Penseur* need not be in harness all day long. He may, like us,
sometimes be pleasantly engaged in just going over the
incidents of yesterday's football match, or the lines of a
well-known poem. Then there is nothing that he is now trying
to achieve, so his occupation can be neither successful nor
unsuccessful. But still he is a little vexed if interrupted. He is
voluntarily and pleasurably strolling; and perhaps he is doing
this strolling in preference to some more profitable or
adventurous travelling. However it would not be by such
unharnessed thinkings that *Le Penseur* would earn his honorific
capital letters.

But now I want to go back to the whole notion of what I have
so far metaphorically dubbed 'Adverbial Verbs'. Obviously no
weight can be put on to the back of this metaphor; nor can any
big dividends be drawn from the linguistic fact that quite often
we can, for example, rephrase 'he hurried over his breakfast' by
'he breakfasted hurriedly'. For one thing, no such simple

paraphrasing is possible for all verbs which I have nominated as adverbial; and it is possible for some verbs which are non-adverbial. Think of my suspect adverb 'songfully'.

So far I have not put much more of an edge on the notion of metaphorical adverbiality than is given by such arguments as that the command 'X' (period) is an unfinished command, and the report 'he was X-ing' is an unfinished report, when 'X' is one of my adverbial verbs. It is not just that there happens not to be, but there could not be such a concrete *per se* activity as just hurrying, obeying, enjoying, playing, persevering, experimenting or taking care, any more than there could be such a concrete *per se* object or entity as a bottom, a middle, a corner, a grin or a half. It is not just a causal 'can', that for example hurrying *can* be in progress only if something concrete such as breakfasting is in progress, where this concrete something else *could* be being done hurriedly, unhurriedly or dawdlingly.

I am going to approach what I hope is my objective by a knight's move. Think first of all not about verbs but about nouns. Lots of our nouns are crudely classifiable as abstract nouns. What do we need abstract nouns for? When we can comfortably declare Socrates to be wise and Simple Simon to be unwise, and Socrates to be wiser than Simple Simon, why do we sometimes discard these comfortably unsophisticated adjectives in favour of the chillingly sophisticated nouns 'wisdom' and 'unwisdom'? Part of the reason is this. Having become quite accustomed to saying at stage one, for instance, that Socrates is wise, was wiser than Simple Simon, will be too wise to lose his temper, and so on, we, at stage two, for a lot of new purposes, to generalize over Socrates and Simple Simon, and also over dates and occasions and to talk of unparticularized people who are on unparticularized occasions wise or unwise, to assert that no one who was wise would so-and-so, and to explain why it would be unwise for anyone ever or often to so-and-so. Our comfortable adjective is still with us, but it is now functioning, still in its regular predicative way, in de-particularized, that is, generalized, sentences and clauses. And now the abstract noun 'wisdom' comes into its own, for it enables us to 'nominalize' not just the adjective 'wise' but the entire de-particularized clauses or sentences in which, at stage two, it had been doing its habitual, but now long-winded, business. Now we are restored to the cosy idiom exemplified by

'Socrates is honest' and can say in the same cosy idiom such things as that 'Honesty is the best policy'. No far-fetched explanation is wanted for our preferring this one-nominative, one-verb idiom, when it becomes available, to the idiom 'whoever is honest, he gains more because he is honest than he loses because he is honest' – a five-claused, five-verbed sentence with five shadow or dummy nominatives in it.

So now I suggest that what I have been calling 'adverbial verbs' are not, of course, *nominalizations* of, but *'verb*-izations' of de-particularized sentences and clauses in which adverbs and adverbial phrases more or less forcefully qualify their now de-particularized verbs. Such stage-two generalizations are very frequently required when there begin such things as training, drill, class-instruction and class-censure, legislation, preaching or character-descriptions. It may be true of, or required of each of the children who are engaged in doing widely differing things, that he is doing or should do *whatever he is doing* assiduously or quietly – and the verbs 'persevere' and 'hush' enable this de-particularized report or command to be given in the cosy old idioms of 'he is digging' or 'dig'. It is the verbization of a range of available but unhandy de-particularized verbed sentences or verbed clauses. For the particular statement 'he was hurrying' to be true, it must be true that he was doing something or other hurriedly; and for this to be true there must have been a particularizable concrete something that he was doing. For the general statement 'he never hurries' to be true, it must be true that whatever he ever does, he does unhurriedly; and for this to be true there must be a range of specifiable concrete things such that when he does any of these specifiable concrete things he does them unhurriedly and if he were to do them he would do such specifiable concrete things unhurriedly. But for certain purposes we do not need to provide, we even need not to provide specifications of, these specifiables.

Sentences verbed by adverbial verbs are, therefore, constitutionally on a higher generality-plane than the first-stage sentences that are verbed with an ordinarily adverbed particularizing verb, i.e. adverbially verbed sentences are at least one sophistication-rung above these first-stage sentences. If no grammarian is listening, I incline to re-dub my 'adverbial verbs' 'abstract verbs', since 'obeyed' stands to (*inter alia*) 'sloped arms' somewhat as 'wisdom' stands to (*inter alia*) 'Socrates'. This, I suggest, shows or begins to show, just why the soldier who obeyed and sloped arms did not do two separately do-able things, however interlockingly. For the report of his obeying embodied, on a higher generality-plane, a gap to be filled either by the specification of sloping arms or by the specification of some other obedient action. There was something specifiable that he did (sloped arms or saluted) on hearing and taking in an order from his sergeant in the parade ground to do it, whatever *it* was – and for many of our purposes it does not matter what in particular *it* was.

I leave to you the application of these ideas to the special notions of thinking, with one suggestion. What was wrong with the Duplicationists or Cartesians, and what was wrong with the Reductionists or Behaviourists (perhaps including one leg and one ear of Ryle himself), was that they both assumed that verbs of attending, trying, applying one's wits, taking care, repeating, experimenting, checking, calculating, deliberating, etc. were verbs on the same specificity-plane as those, for example, of eating, typing, murmuring, fidgeting. Hence the Inner Worldliness of the Cartesians and the Outer Worldliness of the Behaviourists. The former wished to expose to the private light of consciousness, the latter wished to expose to the public light of day, some specified *per se* doings, answering to verbs which are in fact abstract verbs. They construed adverbial verbs as action-specifiers instead of as qualifiers of unspecified but specifiable actions.

So, to wind up, I am suggesting that our titles for the specific things that *Le Penseur* may be engaged in, say, 'calculating', 'composing' or 'examining a would-be proof' belong to the same general class as 'scrutinize', 'bargain' and 'damage' – namely, to the class of those positive or *per se* verbs which already carry some of their own adverbial luggage. But in the case of the verbs that are proprietary to *Le Penseur*, their adverbial luggage is itself many-levelled or many layered. The mistakes that he makes, corrects or avoids, and the obstacles which he overcomes or is defeated by are on a relatively or very high rung of sophistication. He might be trying to diagnose what is temptingly wrong in a fallacious argument from some pieces of evidence extracted by a lawyer from an untrustworthy but technically expert witness. Or he might be a philosopher trying to disentangle the notion of thinking both from the Scylla of Cartesian Duplicationism and the Charybdis of Watsonian or Humean Reductionism – like you and me.

2

Thought and Soliloquy

Partly in healthy demythologizing reaction against Lockean and Humean accounts of thinking, and partly in healthy demythologizing reaction against Meinongian and some Platonic accounts of thinking, many contemporary philosophers say such sweeping things as that Thought is Language, or, with better regard for sense, that thinking is or has to embody saying things to oneself.

In its sweeping form this doctrine is false. Saying things, and therefore saying things to oneself, is not a sufficient or even necessary condition of thinking. A delirious man babbles things but is not thinking; nor am I thinking what I am saying when I have a jingle or a catch-phrase or a ritual formula running in my head or off my tongue. Conversely, the composer at the piano and the child at the jig-saw puzzle are thinking; but they need be saying nothing aloud or to themselves; and if they are saying anything, their saying it probably does no good, and may do some harm. Their solutions to their problems do not reside in what they say, if they happen to say anything; nor are their skills, inefficiency or difficulties linguistic ones. Doubtless when Plato said, in his *Sophist*, that in thinking the soul is conversing with herself, or – I surmise rather – that she is debating with herself, he was considering what he himself did and had to do, when tackling philosophical problems in particular. There are indeed special reasons why, in some special areas, including this one, thinking does require saying things to oneself. Later on I hope we may capture something of what these special reasons are. But for the moment I want to assert dogmatically that just as some games do, but most do not, require playing-cards or dolls' houses, and just as some craftsmen do, but most do not, work with mahogany or with tweed, so some thinking does, but most

thinking does not, require the saying or the sub-saying of anything. If you like – as I do not – to say that *game-playing* is a
'family-likeness concept', then you ought to say – as I shall
not – that *thinking* is also a 'family-likeness concept' and that
saying things to oneself does belong to some, but not to all,
members of the family.

Today, however, I am going to tackle a subordinate issue. For
we certainly do do a lot of saying things to ourselves – perhaps
we academics and especially we philosophical academics do
much more than most people. I want to examine, and examine
suspiciously, this very familiar notion of *saying things to
ourselves* – or rather to examine suspiciously some theoretical
barnacles which have attached themselves to this familiar
notion. The notion itself, though polyhedral, is innocent
enough. But not the barnacles. I nominate straight away two of
these barnacles. One of them is the idea that a person who is
non-absentmindedly and non-gramophonically saying things to
himself is conversing with himself, that is, that soliloquy is
colloquy with one's Alter Ego, or that internal monologue is
dialogue with a cryptic Siamese Twin. In my now repented past
I have myself spoken and written as if this idea was all right. The
other barnacle is the idea that a person who is, with attention
and intention, saying things to himself can and should therefore
be described as thinking *'in'* the words and phrases that he
utters or sub-utters in saying these things to himself – that is, the
idea that as one who talks or writes, talks or writes *in* English,
say, or *in* Chinese, so, in the same sense of 'in', one thinks *'in'*
English or *in* Chinese; or else, what is a different sense of 'in',
that as one who builds, builds *in* brick or concrete, and one who
paints, paints *in* oils or water-colours, so one thinks *in* English or
in Chinese. I shall argue not that in fact one does not do so, but
that this attempted injection after the verb 'to think' of the
preposition *'in'*, taken in either way, is a nonsense-generator.

So now let us look at our familiar notion of saying things to
oneself, and especially, to start with, at the phrase 'to oneself'.
Notice, *en passant*, that a person could be muttering to himself or
humming to himself, or even, I daresay, playing the piano to
himself. Silence is not a *sine qua non*, though if a person is saying
things to himself 'in his head' or humming things 'in his head',
he is then very obviously not saying or humming them to
anyone else, whereas if he is muttering in company, we

eavesdroppers may be in doubt whether he is muttering to his neighbour or muttering to himself.

The leg that the masseur is massaging may be a client's leg, or it may be his own, and the pedestrian's umbrella may be sheltering his wife, or himself, or both. But I cannot literally fence with myself, resuscitate myself, outlive myself, bully, tease or outmanoeuvre myself. Nor can I literally bargain or compete or make a contract with myself, or insult, compliment or trick myself. When did you last blackmail yourself? Well, then, can I literally say things to myself, as I can literally shave myself, or can I only metaphorically say things to myself as I can only metaphorically wrestle with myself? As it stands this question is unanswerable, since, like the phrase 'do things to so and so' there are too many disparate specific things covered by the verbal phrase, 'say things to oneself' for there to be one answer to all of them. We shall, in a moment, do some rummaging among some of these specific things. But first let us look at a half-way-house case.

We look through his caravan window and see the circus clown or the conjuror going through his capers or his prestidigitations in solitude. I suppose we *might*, though I doubt if we really would, say that he is clowning or conjuring to himself, but can he literally be amusing or mystifying himself in the way in which he will be amusing or mystifying the children this evening? Can the quickness of the conjuror's hand be deceiving to the conjuror's eye; or can the clown's practical jokes with the whitewash be taking the clown himself by rapturous surprise? If these entertainers are entertaining themselves, why is there not even a minimally thin cheer from their minimally thin audience? Why are the stage and bright illuminations that are needed in the circus not needed in the caravan? Here there can be no doubt. They are not trying to amuse or mystify an audience, however small. They are, in privacy or by themselves, going through the moves of their tricks, because they are either trying to think up new tricks, or rehearsing their tricks, or both together, in order to be able and ready to amuse or mystify the children when they perform these very same operations this evening. The 'to' in our 'conjuring to himself' does not here mean what it means in the phrase 'to the children', that is, 'in front of the children and for their entertainment'; it means 'by himself' or 'in solitude', and that means *'not* in front of an audience'. Though the clown is now going through his tricks, he is not yet *exhibiting* or *performing* them; he is in solitude *practising* for the public performance of them. Thinly, the moves made in practising may be just like those made in performing, but 'thickly' they, the practise-moves, are different, for they have a different and strictly derivative point or purpose, their canons of success *versus* failure are different; and their required concomitant properties, like footlights and a stage, may be different. Similarly the boxer, shadow-boxing in solitude goes through the motions of giving and parrying blows, yet no blows are given, even to himself, and no blows are parried, even from himself. He makes his shadow-moves this morning to prepare himself for fighting with an opponent this evening. We Paul Prys have no idea what he is up to this morning, unless we know why and how he is preparing himself for a future fight. He has practised inadequately or stupidly this morning if he is unready to hit and parry this evening.

Already we can see by analogy that a person may similarly be saying things to himself, whether in his head or *sotto voce* or aloud, who is just practising saying things now in order to be able and ready to say them to a real audience later on. I am this morning going over my oration for this evening, but I am not orating to a tiny audience, namely to my Alter Ego, this morning, else why do I begin 'Ladies and gentlemen . . .? And why do my jokes elicit no laughter, or my appeals for subscriptions fetch not even a penny from my left-hand pocket? Obviously I am not orating yet – we cannot orate *silently* or *sotto voce*. I am, perhaps in solitude and silence, rehearsing my words for my public oration-to-be. Even if I mutter these words audibly, and you are there to hear them, I am not muttering them for you or for anyone, even for me, to hear them. My rehearsal is not made a failure by your or by my hardness of hearing, but only by my faltering in my delivery of my words at the banquet this evening. Though I am this morning saying things to myself not literally, only in quotes am I 'orating' this morning, and not even in quotes am I speaking to my own receptive or unreceptive ears. I am merely rehearsing by myself. Rehearsing an oration to the Alumni is not rehearsing *to* them or *to* anyone. 'Rehearsing *to* . . .' makes no sense. Well, then, can I literally engage in conversation with myself? Certainly I can, and the dramatist must compose imaginary conversations, perhaps between Romeo and Juliet, or perhaps between Ryle and Ryle's Alter Ego. But while I am concocting, or while I am rehearsing an imaginary conversation, I am not exchanging remarks with anyone, even myself, any more than in shadow-boxing I am exchanging blows with an opponent, not even with an opponent called 'Gilbert Ryle'. Could I, for example, be surprised, intrigued, flattered, offended, mystified or even interrupted by my own interjections? Could I literally ask or tell myself things, consult myself, blab secrets to myself, give mere hints to myself or snub myself? Of course I could, with attention or intention, go through the moves of doing these things in a real conversation. But the 'thick' description of what I am engaged in in going through these moves is not the same as that of what I am engaged in doing in going through these moves in conversation with you. The former description is parasitic on the latter. I am, for example, *preparing*, in solitude, remarks for delivery at the tea-table tomorrow; or I am, for another example, dreaming up remarks which I wish that I had made at the tea-table yesterday. The point, purpose or intention with which I say these things to myself seems, so far, regularly to be obliquely governed by and ancillary to the point, purpose or intention with which I shall or might make them, or could have made them, in proper conversation with proper interlocutors.

You can I think, now see for yourselves, that though I may be going through, in my head, the phrases and sentences of a sermon to a congregation or a lecture to a seminar, I am not preaching or lecturing to a congregation of one or to a seminar of one; I am, perhaps, trying to reconstruct or recapitulate or commit to memory the sermon that I and others heard in a church yesterday; or I am trying to refurbish or condense or expand an old lecture in order to have something to deliver to a real seminar this evening. I do not, for example, docilely take notes on the lecture that I am preparing in my head or on the back of an envelope, as I might of a lecture at which I was present as a listener; nor do I throw my voice to the furthest pews, as I would if I were preaching to a congregation. Rather, I hold my tongue, which I cannot do when preaching. And I begin my inner sermon-recapitulation with 'Dearly beloved brethren' and not with 'Dearly beloved brother, Gilbert'.

In separating off, as parasite from host, some activities of saying things to oneself from those of saying things to others, I am not in the least trying to minimize the importance of the former. On the contrary, I suggest, but for the moment only suggest, that it is precisely here that we are going to find the differentia or one of the differentias of reflective or meditative thinking. It is the very fact that the solitary shadow-boxer is *not* now boxing against an opponent and yet is purposefully and self-coachingly doing *something* that forces us to find a name and a home for the something that he is now engaged in, and for what the composing or the rehearsing orator, musician or conjuror is now engaged in, and for what the undecided chess-player is now engaged in while tentatively making dummy-moves with his queen. All of them are meditating – meditating actions which they are not yet performing, and which, when they are being performed, will not themselves be bits of meditating, that is they will not themselves be parasite-actions but host-actions. But notice that I am not yet asserting that *all* cases of purposively saying things to ourselves are in all or in most ways like the one I nave so far described. But still it is an interesting and I think important fact that if Rodin's *Le Penseur* while sitting on his rock is saying things to himself, with attention and intention, the thinking or meditating in which he is absorbed may be, though it need not be, of one of these kinds. I think we all *hope* that his meditations are profounder and more exploratory or constructive than those of a man merely composing a speech or merely going over, in his head, a poem or sermon already composed, or merely meditating a chess-move. But still he really would qualify as meditating or reflecting even if this were all he was doing. Low-grade meditating is still meditating.

Of the at present fairly new specific kinds of things that I have selected as cases of a person saying things to himself, with attention and intention, some of them differ from some of the others in their specific purposes, and so in what will or would count as their being successful or unsuccessful if the conjuror, when performing his trick before an audience this evening performs it readily and smoothly enough to mystify the children; the corresponding thing holds of tonight's orator who is this morning rehearsing his speech, or the actor rehearsing his part, or the boxer shadow-boxing. But the task of composing a new trick, a new poem, or a new speech is different; the composer is trying to think of something new, and not yet trying to get by heart what has already been composed. The composer fails if he does not complete his poem or speech, or if he completes it, but completes it badly. So he may get perfectly by heart a poor poem, or he may compose a good poem but fail to get it at the tip of his tongue. Hesitating composingly and meditating self-practisingly are different things; their successes and failures are different, and can be independent. The composer need not apologize for his poem, while apologizing for his faltering delivery of it.

It is worth while, at this point, reminding ourselves of Aristotle's ever neglected point, that some purposive doings are not done *for* a purpose, that is for an ulterior purpose. A boxer would, I imagine, hardly ever engage in shadow-boxing except in order to prepare himself for subsequent fighting; but the swimming's sake is to sell a verbal pass to the illusion that all river, to win a race or to show a novice how to swim, might equally well swim not for any of these ulterior purposes, but because he likes swimming. He is then not swimming for the sake of anything – even to say that he is swimming for swimming's sake is to sell a verbal pass to the illusion that all things done on purpose must be done for some ulterior object. Correspondingly then *Le Penseur* might be running over a poem or a piece of music, whether his own or someone else's, not rehearsingly, i.e. not in order to get it better by heart, but just because he likes doing it. Much walking is walking in order to get somewhere, or to work up an appetite, or for health's sake. But sometimes we just go for a walk, and we do not regard the expenditure of energy as wasted if we do not reach any special destination, or if we become no hungrier than we would have been otherwise, or if our health is unimproved, since it was perfect before we set out. Yet just taking a walk *is* doing something on purpose; we are vexed if it is interrupted, and we may have to choose between going for a walk and reading a book. Well, in a similar way, some of our meditatings such as day-dreaming, reverie, and going over in memory the events of yesterday's football match, are not engaged in as investments, searches, preparations or exercises. Though they are directed towards no results, still we may be vexed by an interrruption. If *Le Penseur* did not look so anguished, we could conjecture that he was engaged in just such a piece of intellectual strolling. If saying things to himself, he might, for example, be just effortlessly putting into words some already familiar factual or fictional story; or just re-savouring a joke that went down so well at last night's banquet. Then there would be nothing that he is now trying to accomplish; yet an interruption vexes him.

Before starting off on a partly new task, I want to get two things out of the way. The first is what I call 'the doodling phenomenon'. The committee-member who is totally absorbed in the business finds to his surprise when the committee adjourns, that his fingers and pencil have inscribed a picture or pattern on the blotting paper. He had not meant to draw, say, a giraffe straddling an isosceles triangle, yet there it is. He is neither proud nor ashamed of his craftsmanship, since he has not tried to draw what, in a thin sense, he has drawn. Notice, here, that though doodling is not drawing, since it is not intentional, only a person who can draw can doodle. Doodling is a hangover from drawing.

I am going to extend the coverage of this verb 'doodle'. A person who can and often does hum or whistle tunes on purpose, trying to hum or whistle them correctly, may, to his surprise, notice or be told that he had been humming or whistling a bit or 'Rule Britannia' while he had been totally absorbed in something else. This is musical doodling, and can be a great nuisance to the doodler's companions. In the same way, people, we ourselves, who can and constantly do say things, to others and to ourselves, on purpose and with some degree of care, may catch ourselves doing some purposeless verbal doodling, under our breaths or in our heads. We do this especially when falling asleep, but we do a good deal of it also when wide-awake. The corresponding thing is true of our visualizing or seeing things in our mind's eyes. It has been an historical disaster that epistemologists and psychologists like Hume have taken mental doodlings, verbal and pictorial, as the primary or original sort of thinking and tried then, of course in vain, to account for all thinking as more or less elaborate mental doodling. They might just as well have tried to explain intentional, trained and careful drawing in terms of what we absent-mindedly inscribe on the blotting paper in the committee-room, trying to make the source as derivative from its own hangover. Anyhow, for our purpose, I just mention the fact that sometimes we do, in the thinnest possible sense, 'say' things to ourselves doodlingly, without attention, intention, trying, care, relevance, point, interest, success or failure. This sort of hangover 'saying' is no more telling than is the 'saying' that the delirious babbler does. Just as there is no such thing as *interrupting* delirious babbling, so there is no such thing as *interrupting* doodling. Only what is attempted can be thwarted.

The second thing that I want to clear out of the way is the obsessive philosophical notion of 'thinking *in*', such as thinking *in* words or pictures. I shall deal only with the notion that thinking or some thinking needs to be described as thinking *in* words, or thinking *in* English. Take the will-be orator composing his speech. It is to be a speech in English, so of course he has tentatively and experimentally to think up English words and phrases, consider these, reject a lot of them, modify others, string together the selected or provisionally selected candidates into sentences, paragraphs and finales. His speech, when made, will of course be in English. Perhaps while composing his speech the word 'apolaustic' occurs to him, so he considers it and rejects it as too pompous, or because he is not sure what it means. He thought it up, the thought about it and he scrapped it for a reason. But surely we cannot say that his thinking was *'in'* this rejected word? What of the phrases and sentences that finally constitute his speech? Had he thought *in* them while composing? Obviously not. He had then been searching for them, and his searching could no more be described as *in* its objectives than prospecting could be described as being done *in* diamonds or *in* nuggets of gold. In some cases then, it makes no sense to say that even the thinker who is indeed saying things to himself in English or French words and phrases is thinking *in* these words or phrases – or anything else instead.

Take one more case, that of the translator who is trying to render into German a passage from Gibbon's *Decline and Fall of the Roman Empire*. Gibbin's sentences are on the page in front of the translator's nose. The translator is not composing *them*; Gibbon has done that. But of course the translator has to read Gibbon's words and try to understand them. Next, the translator is having to think up not just any German words, phrases and sentences, but just those which will do for the particular job, that of conveying precisely what Gibbon's words convey. So if you want to say that he is thinking *in* words, phrases and sentences, are you going to say that he is thinking *in* Gibbonian English, or *in* would-be Gibbonian German, or *in* both? Really, of course, he is thinking *about* Gibbon's words and style, experimentally thinking up German words and constructions and thinking censoriously *about* these *vis à vis* those of Gibbon. The preposition 'in' has no place – but of course his final product is in German, for it is a translation into German.

Consider together these people – Gibbon composing the passage, a schoolboy trying to memorize the passage, maybe without understanding much of it, the translator trying to translate the passage. Then the third sentence, say, of the passage will very likely have been said, in his head maybe, by Gibbon, the boy and the translator. Yet, as what they were severally engaged in were different tasks, governed by quite different success-conditions, their thinking were disparate thinkings. If an eavesdropper overheard each of them muttering, say, 'the battle despatched more Christians to heaven than infidels to hell' he could, as yet, tell us nothing about the similarities or differences between their intellectual labours. But enough of 'thinking in English or in German'.

Now I want to move on to a different sort of point. What I have said so far about the relations between *some* thinking and saying things to oneself, is open to the objection that I have not tackled the notion of *real* thinking. It may be conceded that all that *Le Penseur may* be doing is, say, composing an after-dinner speech, or trying to memorize or translate a passage from Gibbon, and that such tasks do qualify as meditating or thinking of a not very grand sort. But *Le Penseur* would not qualify as a Thinker with a capital T, just for engagement, however proficient, in tasks like these. What we want of the high-grade thinker is that he be a Thinker of Thoughts – and neither the will-be orator, the memorizer or the translator qualifies, unless *per accidens*, as a Thinker of Thoughts. The after-dinner speech may be a good speech, the translation may be a good translation, without their recipients becoming any the wiser. They will not have been taught any new truths or been brought abreast of any new advances in astronomy, geometry, theology, history or philosophy. *Le Penseur*, if he is to merit his capital letter, ought to be some sort of intellectual explorer or researcher, and what he is, at any given moment, saying to himself (non-doodlingly, of course), ought to be a contribution, somehow, to his truth-hunt.

Or perhaps we should enlarge this requirement a bit. For we should not cease to venerate *Le Penseur* if his thinkings, when successful, resulted not in new truths, but in new policies of statesmanlike or strategic dimensions. He will qualify not only if he is an Euclid, a Newton or a Kant, but also if he is a Nelson, a Gladstone or even a Henry Ford.

The composing orator, essayist or translator is indeed thinking, but he is trying to decide only what to say and how to say it; *Le Penseur*, we hope, is doing something of a different order, namely trying to make up his mind what to *think*. It may be that usually, if not quite always, trying to decide what to think also involves trying to decide how to express things. The intellectual explorer is not exempted from all rhetorical or literary tasks by the fact that his primary task is not itself a rhetorical or literary one. Kant is not, though Hume is, a very good writer, but the lack of the possession of this virtue does not, by itself, determine whether either is a bad or a good philosopher. Total inarticulateness would prevent a person from being anything at all of an historian; but articulateness is not enough to make him one. A theoretical physicist's mistake is not corrected by perfecting its expression; he needs to take some pains over his expression, but more or different pains to avoid or correct mistakes or theory.

I am not about to lay bare what is to be an intellectual explorer. But I do want at least to nibble at the ancillary issue, which belongs to my theme for this evening, of what sort, or, more likely, what sorts, of things are done by the Thinker (with a capital 'T') in saying, muttering or scribbling things to himself, without which he would not even be trying to make up his mind what to think.

Let us start at a very low level. Take first the child who can now, without hesitations or mistakes, rattle off to himself in his head or aloud, the series of number-words 'One, two, three . . .' and go as far as he likes. Now he has to master a new sort of task, namely that of *counting* things. All he is asked to do is, for example, to find out how many people are in the room, say seventeen. Before he can give us or himself this correct, or even some other incorrect answer, he must indeed run through, aloud or in his head, the number-words in their due sequence, but he must also, so to speak, pin each of them in succession to each of his victims in succession. He has miscounted if he pins on to one victim two or more successive number-words, or pins on to two or more successive victims the same number-word. And of course he has not counted them all, if he just shuts his eyes and rattles off the number-words, like letters of the alphabet, and stops, from fatigue, at the number seventeen. Obviously his task of counting the seventeen people requires at a certain stage, namely the sixth stage, saying or sub-saying the number 'six', plus, of course pinning it on to his sixth victim. But we, who have asked him how many people there are, do not need or want (unless for pedagogic purposes) to hear him sing out the number 'six'. He has to say it, but not for *our* sake. His saying it, even if he is saying it audibly, has not got a conversational point. It makes no difference if we fail to hear it. Nor does he say it just for fun. His purpose in saying it, whether aloud or in his head is an *heuristic* purpose, that is in order eventually to find out how many people are in the room. It is like a rung of a ladder – not there for exhibition, or as a thing to stand on, but as a thing to step on to and to step off in order to get to the destination, where the top of the ladder is. Or, to change the illustration, it is like a stepping-stone in a river for people who want to be on the far side of the river – its sole function being that of enabling people to get past it to where they want to be. It is not itself where they want to be; but it is a necessary step in getting where they want to be.

As a half-digression, suppose the boy is asked how many hockey-players are on the field: he tries to count them, but as they are running about he cannot pin his number-words on to them. His difficulty is not a vocabulary-difficulty; he is not having to think what number succeeds the number five. He can run through his English number-words fast and correctly. Shall we say that he is trying in vain to count in English the hockey players, when nothing in his stock of English is what baffles him? Somewhat as spelling requires but does not reduce to mastery of the alphabet, so counting requires but does not reduce to mastery of the series of number-words. Neither a spelling-mistake nor a counting-mistake *is* a slip in the recitation of the alphabet or of the number-series. Is Tommy in carefully reciting the alphabet through M N O P Q R S T thinking *in* the letter Q? Is Sarah in misspelling 'Quick' with two Q's thinking *in* the letter Q? And are their problems identical, just because uttering Q occurs in their engaging in their two separate tasks?

Now come to the slightly grander task of calculating, say

multiplying. Obviously one cannot multiply if one cannot count, any more than one can count without knowing the series of numbers. But a success or mistake in multiplying is not a success or mistake in counting. So, although the number-word forty-seven, say, occurs in what is said to himself by the child reciting his numbers, by the child counting people, and by the child multiplying three pounds forty-seven pence by three, what the three children are trying to do is quite different. And let us notice one special difference between counting people and multiplying three pounds forty-seven pence by three. The child counting nominated 'six' to himself in its due attachment to the sixth victim, and his saying this was a necessary step towards his reaching the completion of his count. But for the multiplier the necessary steps, or some of them, are not controlled number-nominations, but complete equations. 'three times seven are twenty-one; put down one and carry twenty; three times forty are one pound twenty; one pound twenty and twenty are one pound forty; put down forty and carry one' and so on. His stepping stones are arithmetical statements or propositions, hopefully true ones. For him too, even if he works out his calculations aloud, his stepping-stone statements have no conversational or didactic point, but only an heuristic point. They have done their job of enabling the mulitplier to get his answer, even if the companion who wants the answer has misheard or failed to hear the muttered steps; or even if the steps have not been muttered aloud, but only said to himself by the multiplier. The same sort of things, though not the same things can be said of the thinking which is trying to construct a proof of something or an argument for or against something. The thinker, Euclid, say, or , what is very different, Sherlock Holmes, is stepping or trying to step *via* stated paths, or at least *via* stated truth-candidates to the far bank, namely to the establishing of a proposition. His interim or step-statements have, here and now, only an heuristic point, for all that when originally propounded, say by the witness in the witness box, their whole point had then been an information-imparting point or, sometimes, a mis-information-imparting point. The witness would have been unsuccessful if his testimony had been unheard or misheard. But for the objectives of Sherlock Holmes or Euclid in thinking up their arguments, it is immaterial whether their step-statements are or could be heard by a

listener. They are not being said for *his* sake but to enable their
employers to get somewhere, and to get there by due process.
As spelling did not reduce to reciting the alphabet, as counting
did not reduce to reciting the number-series, and as multiplying
did not reduce to counting, so argument-constructing does not
reduce to statement-making. Committing a fallacy, though it is
making a mistake, is not making one or several false statements.

Well, to wind up with, Euclid and Sherlock Holmes, in
constructing their arguments, are certainly saying things to
themselves. But what they say to themselves are not remarks
with a conversational point, but propositions with an heuristic
point – indeed this is already hinted by the occupational word
'proposition'. Only in jest would we, in reporting a conversation
between Queen Victoria and her daughter, say that the Queen
propounded three dozen propositions. Remarks, complaints,
retorts, and so on are not propostions until they are employed as
such and when so employed they are no longer remarks,
complaints or retorts, – or if you like, only dead ones. Nor is a
cricket-bat handle a rung in a ladder until it is so
employed – and then it is no longer a cricket-bat handle – or
only a dead one.

Here, I suggest, we have an approach, but only an approach,
to what the Thinker with a capital T, the thinker of thoughts, is,
or at lease could be, engaged in that Queen Victoria or the
after-dinner speaker-to-be are not engaged in. These latter do
indeed compose significant sentences in the indicative mood,
and what they say, aloud or to themselves, is, by and large, true
or false. Nonetheless, in saying these things they are not trying
to decide what to think. Their meditated remarks or their
perorations are not said or therefore manipulated with an
heuristic intention. Queen Victoria is composing a snub, and the
composing orator is composing a subscription-extractor. But
Euclid, Sherlock Holmes, Gibbon and Kant are working at a
higher level, or, of you like, a deeper level; if successful they will
have found something that, thenceforward, they and their
hearers or readers will know, which they did not know before,
but needed to know.

You grumble that I have not yet done justice to the thinkings
of the philosopher, the prophet, the genius, the mystic or the
sage, I reply, 'Well, just give me time – a century or two.'
Before closing down I want to take stock of part of what I have

been doing or trying to do. I want first to bring out a general future to the general notion of *doing* so and so, and then to apply the result to the special notion of *saying* so and so. We see a boy running towards the edge of a stream, launching himself into the air and coming down either on the far bank or else in the stream. What is he doing? To begin with we suppose that he was trying to get to the far side of the stream dry-shod, and that he has either succeeded or failed in his undertaking. But then we see him turn round and jump back again, and he repeats this several times. So perhaps he is just practising jumping. This idea is a bit confirmed if we then see him jumping over the garden path and back again, over the tennis-net and back again. He is just trying to make himself better at jumping over streams, paths or no-matter-what. But then we notice that he jumps and rejumps over no-matter-what only when someone else is watching him, and is annoyed when a jump is unwitnessed. So apparently he has been jumping not, or not only, to improve his performance, but either vaingloriously to elicit admiration or else didactically to demonstrate to inferior jumpers the *how* of jumping. Or, if he jumps in a ludicrously awkward manner he is, in order to amuse, parodying the jumping of a despised schoolmaster, and is peevish if his companions either look elsewhere or do not notice the fact that he is jumping parodyingly, or are unamused by the parody. So our original 'thin' description of him as trying to jump the stream is compatible with a wide range of alternative 'thick' descriptions, that is descriptions of what he is trying to do, and so of what counts or would count as his successes, failures, skills and inefficiencies, obstacles and interruptions. But there is more than mere compatibility. For the thick descriptions all essentially embody oblique mentions of what is given in the thin descriptions. What, if practising, he is trying to do is to make himself better at *jumping* – not at practising jumping; what, if demonstrating, he is trying to do is to teach someone else how to *jump* – not how to teach jumping. And what, if parodying his schoolmaster, he is trying to do is to simulate the schoolmaster *jumping* – not parodying jumping.

This relation between the thickly described actions and the thinly described actions is often nowadays dubbed the relation of being 'parasitic on'. (The pejorative connotations of the adjective should be ignored.) We could not think of a jump as a simulation, a piece of practice, a self-advertisement, or a didactic demonstration unless we already knew what it is for someone to jump over something – any more than we could think of a mental disc as a counterfeit coin, unless we already had the idea of money; or think of someone obeying the order to slope arms unless we already had the idea of sloping arms. These former ideas stand to the latter as parasites to hosts. Such parasitisms can escalate. The child may be doing his five-finger exercises on the piano not because he is trying to improve, but because he has been told to do it – so he gladly stops when his mentor is called away; and he does not perform these exercises when his mentor forgets to tell him to do them. Or he may be trying to do two things at once, namely both to obey his mentor and to improve his playing. He does just a little practising, even in the absence of his mentor, and feels just a bit discontented if he fumbles even when his mentor does not notice. But he might be experimentally disobeying his mentor's command to stop practising, just in order to see how his flouted mentor reacts.

Notice that practising jumping, demonstrating jumping, and parodying jumping do not *reduce* to jumping. An unsuccessful jump terminates in a wetting; unsuccessful practice jumps result in no long-term improvement at jumping; unsuccessful parody-jumps result in no malicious laughter. The parasites *are* not their hosts. The thin description enters into each of the rival thick descriptions, but does not exhaust them.

It is easy to see now that the notion of saying so-and-so is, in the same ways, parasite-hospitable. The child who merely tries to echo my 'the mouse ran up the clock' succeeds or fails if he achieves or fails to achieve phonetic fidelity. 'Hickory, Dickory, Dick' is just as good an exercise in echoing. If he gets the echoing wrong or incomplete, he is inclined to try again. But the child who, when asked what ran up the clock, or where the mouse ran, says 'the cat' or 'the mouse ran up the clock' is or may be doing more. He has got the story wrong or right, and not just the noise. He cannot tell me or mis-tell me the story without uttering strings of phonemes. But he is not trying only to utter correctly a string of phonemes.

The child who wants to be the first teller of a surprising incident, say, that a mouse ran up the clock, is disappointed if his hearer knows it already, or disbelieves the story. Or, if a bit more sophisticated, he may be trying to get his hearer to swallow a fabrication, and is disappointed if his yarn is received with scepticism. At a higher level still of sophistication, he may say the same old thing in explanation of the stopping of the clock, or as evidence for the mouse's ingenuity. Later still he may say the same thing, protasis-wise or apodosis-wise, when asked for a possible explanation of something or a possible premise for some possible conclusion, or *vice versa*. This crude ladder of sophistication-rungs is a crude ladder of parasite sayings that are all, in different ways, parasitic on the host saying of the phonemes 'the mouse ran up the clock'. The mere correct parroting of this string of phonemes is an infantile accomplishment, whereas saying 'The mouse runs up the clock when the cat mews' is reporting a true or false induction. The child stands corrected when told 'not always'. Is this induction-report reducible to the phoneme-parroting? Obviously not. Is the first half of the induction-report the saying of something that was not said in the phoneme-parroting? Well, not necessarily. It depends with what load the word 'said' is said. Clarity about what *Le Penseur* is or may be doing requires clarity about the sophistication-level of the doing, for example the saying, that he is or may be engaged in. It is a gross error in one direction to say that *Le Penseur* is, for instance *just* saying things. It is a gross error in the other direction to say that since he is not *just* saying things, he is therefore doing something else as well. The child who experimentally disobeys the order to stop practising his five-finger exercises, was continuing to do five-finger exercises. But he was not *just* doing five-finger exercises; nor yet was he doing something else that was do-able separately from these exercises. What made his experiment a successful or unsuccessful experiment was not what made his five-finger exercises deft or clumsy finger-movements. Nor, if *Le Penseur's* worded ponderings are successful, does this success reduce to phonetic fidelity, reportorial accuracy, informative surprisingness, grammatical correctness, stylistic elegance, or probably sleuthlike clue-following. He is, very likely, on a still higher sophistication-rung. He might, for example, be like ourselves, thinking about thinking.

3

Thought and Imagination

There are some contexts and situations (1) in which it comes natural to us to treat thought and imagination as diametrical opposites, as work is opposite to play. (2) In other contexts and situations we are inclined to treat them as merely different, as cricket is different from football. (3) But there remain some other contexts and situations in which we regard a person's thinking and imagination as part and parcel of one another – his thinking is imaginative thinking, or his imaginings are coherent considered imaginings. Let me illustrate.

(1) A mother, distraught with anxiety for her child who is missing from home, imagines all sorts of possible and impossible contingencies. Too distraught to consider evidence or probabilities, she is the passive victim of dreadful fantasies, which pursue one another without rhyme or reason, and are quite outside her control. Her imagination is feverishly active, and her powers of thinking are in abeyance. She has lost her head.

(2) A man reading a scientific account of the physical geography of Lapland follows carefully what he is told, but fills out the scientific account of the land with mental pictures of what the scenery might be like or romances about how the inhabitants make their living, and so on. He is both thinking like a student of physical geography, and composing like a scenario writer. He dramatizes what he is learning without necessarily in any measure distorting it.

(3) The historian or detective in trying to work out a problem needs to be both fertile in hypotheses and careful about his evidence, his chronology, and his railway time tables. He has to realize quickly and in lively detail what would or could have been the concrete filling of each hypothesis with the calendar, with the railway timetable and with the humdrum probabilities

51

of every day affairs. He must think imaginatively and he must imagine consistently, methodically and unfancifully.

When we begin to reflect on these and other differences and connections between thought and imagination we are still liable to have our movements hampered by the old fashioned but not yet moribund notion that a man, or a man's Mind is divisible into faculties, and that his intellect is one such department and his imagination is another. So we vaguely suppose that he may be exercising his intellect for ten minutes, and then exercising his imagination for the next ten minutes, and then if he is mentally ambidextrous enough perhaps he may manage to exercise them both together for a few minutes. We may even go on when in this mood and treat his memory, his sentience, his sense of humour and his conscience as four additional faculties, each of which can be given its own separate exercises. But this picture of a man's mind as being something like the War Office, comprising lots of semi-autonomous departments, having sometimes little and sometimes much to do with one another, is pure mythology. It is I who remember or forget, I who calculate and infer, I who smell and hear things, I who invent fairy stories, I who feel pangs of guilt, and so on. It is not mysterious bits of my mind that do these things for me, in the way in which my solicitor or my chimney sweep or my electric oven do things for me. I do these things and it is because I do them in the ways in which I do them that I am described as having a mind of such and such a sort.

There are two other theoretical obsessions that can get in our way. When considering abstract questions about the intellect we are apt to treat arithmetical computation as its most typical exercises – as if the best thinkers in their best moments are doing in their heads the sort of things that computing machines do, only much faster, in their complex insides. I don't know where this superstition comes from. Computation is, though very important, so low a form of thinking that a well trained cashier can do lengthy and complex computations while thinking about something else. Moreover pure computation-tasks offer no scope whatsoever for originality, talent, flair, horse sense, taste, judiciousness in the weighing of evidence, or constructiveness in the building up of chains of argumentation. Most of those very qualities of intellect which we prize most highly have no scope whatsoever in tasks of adding, multiplying and dividing. Near idiots can be calculating prodigies. I am not of course talking about mathematical enquiries proper, but only about those computing operations in which we were drilled at school, merely adding, subtracting, multiplying and dividing.

There is another prevalent obsession, this time an obsession about imagination. People often talk as if a person's imagination was exercised only in romancing, that is in dreaming up fictional things and happenings. Now of course, Charles Dickens, say, did have a wonderful imagination, and he did invent a world of fictional people, and fictional incidents. But Edison had a good imagination too; yet what he invented were gadgets, appliances and such like which were very often manufactured the moment they were invented. Dickens' Mr. Pickwick is an imaginery character; but the electric light bulb and the telephone are not imaginery appliances, though the inventing of them required a combination of imagination with technical know-how. Nor are the details of, say, the destruction of the Spanish Armada fictional just because the historian who narrates the story tells it in vivid imaginative prose and not just in tables of statistics.

Take another sort of case. When a particular Rugby football player is praised for playing imaginatively, he is not being praised for dreaming up football games or football situations from his arm chair. He is being praised for things of this sort: in trying to get past the opposing fullback, he does not employ the same swerve or jink time after time – or maybe he does do so five times just in order to surprise him on the sixth occasion by a quite different manoeuvre. Nor does he assume that his own centre forward is going to pass out to the left this time, as he did the last three times. He is ready for it to come his way this time. He realizes swiftly that there is the chance of a gap opening up at a place where, at the moment, it looks as though there is going to be no such opening. And so on. He is ready and quick to anticipate, to recognize and to act on things which are out of the rut. He surprises his opponents and is not himself taken by surprise. He exploits the un-routine. But all this has nothing to do with whether he also composes, so to speak, football fairy-stories as a private hobby.

So now let us try to pick out some of the genuine and authentic features which distinguish relatively unimaginative from relatively imaginative thinking.

Let us compare two biographers each of whom has written a

life of Napoleon. Both have worked hard, studied the available evidence, visited the fields of battle, and so on. Both have worked out well-organized and coherent accounts of Napoleon's strategies, tactics, supplies, staff-organizations, etc. Neither biography is a mere assemblage of undigested scraps of evidence. Both our historians have thought out their biographies. Yet one of them fails, where the other succeeds, in making Napoleon, his soldiers, his women and his campaigns come to life. Neither biography contains a word of fiction; yet one of them is conspicuously unimaginative where the other is conspicuously imaginative. What is this contrast?

From the quite efficient but unimaginative biographer we learn what, of course we do need to learn: how long the battle of, say, Waterloo lasted, how much ammunition was expended, and how big the casualties were. From the quite efficient but also imaginative biographer we learn these things too, but, so to speak, we also smell the gunpowder and we also hear the horses' hooves squelching in the mud of the sunken Belgian road. The former biographer duly classifies the weather in meteorologically correct terms, as a heavy and steady downpour; the other also personally acquaints us with the weather, by describing the riflemen's water-filled boots, and their rain-soaked rations. The one gives us meteorological cheques where the other gives us the meteorological goods. The one tells us things that we need to know, but the other does more in also making us realize them.

His imagining is not or rather need not be a rival or a supplanter of his thinking. He thinks in a concrete and not merely in an abstract way; or he thinks in a dramatic and not merely in a schematic way; or he thinks in a participant's and not merely in a statistician's way. He is not exercising two faculties any more than is the landscape painter who not only represents the shapes and sizes and positions of the trees and rocks, but also depicts their colours and shades.

However we have to allow that our imaginative biographer does run a perpetual risk from which his unimaginative confrère is exempt. He will be under a constant temptation to let his fancy escape from the harness of the evidence. Having the interests and the skills of a Daniel Defoe or a Tolstoy or a Stendhal he is tempted to forget that his task is also an historian's and not only a romancer's task.

Even so the fact that a deliberate romancer like Defoe or Dickens is not engaged in historical research by no means involves that he is not thinking at all. Certainly he is not thinking out an historian's questions in the light of an historian's evidence. His romance is not meant to be a contribution to historical knowledge. But still it has to be, say, a coherent and consecutive story; the characters have to be in some degree credible characters and even if its scenes are laid in fairyland this land must not be a lunatic land. If the writer write in prose his prose has to be grammatical prose; his sentences have to be linked by connectives; and his paragraphs have to prepare the way for their successors. Romancing does not oust thinking – it is a special kind of thinking– though not a kind dedicated to the increase of knowledge. It is not academic thinking or laboratory thinking, or Sherlock Holmes thinking. And it is very patently not computer thinking. But it is novelist's thinking.

I hope that by now the temptation to which we are all subject, to *contrast* thinking with imagination is diminishing. There remains, of course, the need to fix more definitely the nature of the differences between relatively unimaginative and relatively imaginative thinking. In order to do this let us first of all consider one or two special kinds of thinking where there is no place at all for the exercise of the imagination in order to see why there is no such place. As I have indicated there is no place at all or almost no place for it in doing bits of multiplication, or long division. If a schoolboy's terminal report described his multiplication as imaginative, original, adventurous, creative or inventive it would describe it as very bad. Similarly there is no place for imagination in the task of accurately translating flat commercial or scientific prose from English into French, while there *is* room for some imagination in the task of translating an English novel into French; and any amount of room for imagination, originality and creativeness in the task of translating English poetry into French poetry. Why these differences? We can, I hope, clear up our still blurred notion of imagination by considering differences like these.

The task of doing a piece of multiplication is one in which each step is preordained by our schoolmasters. First multiply the seven by the three, write down one and carry two, then multiply the five by the three, and add the two . . . and so on, and so on. At each step by itself there is no room for option or invention or preference. Seven times three *is* twenty-one – no thought of any other number need or should occur. One number is right and all the rest would be wrong. There is no place for ingenuity or sagacity; no place for considerations of elegance, economy, fertility or outside chances. The whole chain of operations is a series of drill evolutions. Initiative, adventurousness, inventiveness, and exploratoriness are as bad qualities here as they are on the barrack square. The task, if difficult at all, is only difficult because it is wearisome and dull. The same is true of translations of flat commercial or scientific prose. For each English word the counterpart French word must be supplied. For each grammatical construction the counterpart French construction must be supplied. Here too the task is only difficult because it is dull. Machines already cope with this kind of translation, just as other machines can give the correct change for a fifty pence piece. By contrast, in the task of rendering a piece of English fiction and still more a piece of English poetry into French we can do comparatively little in the way of applying inculcated drills. Here we do not know what to do until we have thought what to do, and the thinking involves trying new things out for the first time and then criticizing these attempts; inventing things and then testing our own inventions to destruction, considering hopefully what might do the trick and then considering suspiciously whether this does do the trick. The moves that we make are not preordained. This sort of task is difficult and sometimes complete success is unattainable. But the work is not dull for it is not and cannot be hackneyed work, or work for which a rigid routine suffices.

We may incline to put the difference in this way. In multiplying and in translating flat technical prose we have no freedom of action. The thing to be done at each step is fixed by the computing drill in the one case and by the dictionary of equivalents in the other. But in these other cases we have some freedom of action. Our next move is not blue-printed for us. This is true but it must not be exaggerated. The translator of the English poem cannot put down anything that freshly occurs to him. He may put down only that one of all the fresh options that have occurred to him which helps most to secure a translation as near perfect as possible. The translator has not got the freedom of action of the composer of the poem – and the composer himself could not be a verbal libertine or crank. Nearer, I think, to the heart of the matter than this negative notion of unshackledness, are the positive notions of inventing, essaying, having a shot and exploring. In translating a poem, as in getting across an unbridged watercourse, we have to think up for ourselves and then suspiciously try out possible ways of getting where we want to be – and the solutions to these problems are not things that can be got from a book or fetched up out of a store of things previously memorized. For we have never been here before; our schoolmasters were never here before; very likely no one in the wide world has ever been here before. Nor even could we have been taught any general rules or recipes or tricks, by the simple applications of which the right solution or even some promising solution-candidates can be automatically constructed. We have to originate or innovate, and we cannot innovate by following learned precedents or by applying established recipes.

In greatly differing degrees we all have many varieties of inventiveness in us. For example we all make from time to time casual little jokes of our own which are not pure repetitions of previously made jokes. They may not be very good jokes. But they are *new* ones. Notice, now, that if asked how you came to think of the joke that you made just now you are stumped for an answer. For we have no recipe or technique or way of joke making, or if, like Oscar Wilde, we do have such a recipe, it does not by itself generate just *this* new joke. So we vaguely say, 'Oh! it just came to me.' We have no answer to the question 'How?', that is to the question 'By what method?' or 'By what procedure?' Similarly if suddenly or after much toil and after the rejection of many failures the translator of the poem hits on a phrase which does the trick he has no answer to give to the question, 'How did you think of it?' There was no 'How', no generalized procedure, no tram rail. Yet the previous practice that he had had in translating, the work that he had put in on this particular poem, the criticisms that he had received, the failures of others that he had himself criticized – all these went into his being able and ready to have the wanted phrase 'just come to him' and to recognize it when it came to him. Inventing and discovering are not techniques, but they are not magic either. Sometimes there are ways – though seldom drilled ways – of searching; and there are methods for testing whether we have found what we are searching for. But the hitting on what we have been searching for is a success – and very often there is no way of making sure in advance that the search will be successful. Very, very often it is unsuccessful, so when we have no answer to the question, 'How did you hit on the wanted phrase?' or the timely joke or the mechanical invention. Yet very often we know that it was not by mere luck. We discriminate between the drilled thinking of the computer and the thinking of the joker or the translator of a poem or the inventor by saying, quite correctly, that there is no room for imagination in the former and lots of room for imagination in the latter. And what there is room for in the latter has something to do with these notions of origination, invention, improvisation, discovery, innovation, exploration, experimentation, of knowingly leaving the beaten track.

But we are not at our destination yet. (1) A minor point. Edison, I believe, invented scores or hundreds of gadgets and appliances. He was imaginatively brisk, energetic, resourceful and fertile. But we might still want to grade him lower in respect of his powers of imagining than someone else – Faraday, perhaps or Archimedes – who made relatively few inventions or discoveries. For these few inventions or discoveries might be much greater innovations, much greater departures from the already envisaged, than all those of Edison's put together.

The poet Tennyson wrote a very great number of lines of poetry, most of which show some talent, some freshness of word-combination, some metrical dexterity. (Some of them of course rise much higher than this). But we might well wish to rank Tennyson's composing genius lower than that of Sappho, say, or Keats, who wrote in comparison only a small number of lines. For the inventive powers of Sappho or Keats might outclass that of Tennyson despite the fact that their products were outnumbered by those of Tennyson – just as a man who made a very few very good jokes might deserve to be ranked higher than a man who made a great number of only moderately good jokes. Discoveries, inventions, innovations can differ in magnitude as well as in number. A man who makes a bridge across one very wide river may be a greater bridge builder than one who makes bridges over a hundred narrow rivers. Edgar Wallace wrote scores of novels and Jane Austen finished only six; yet Edgar Wallace had a limited imagination, where Jane

Austen's imagination gave to the novel and thence to the biography a complete new dimension.

(2) To return to the distinction between my two biographers of Napoleon, of whom the first lacked the imaginative powers that were possessed by the second, we want to say that the superior imaginativeness of the second biographer had something intimately to do with his ability to think and so to write in concrete, graphic and specific terms. He did not content himself, as the other biographer did, with saying that it rained two and a half inches in twelve hours; he brought this two and a half inches rain to literacy and historical life by describing the riflemen's waterfilled boots and their soggy midday rations constituting local and personal details, which though authenticated historical facts, never occurred to the first biographer as worthy of being looked for, mentioned or written about. He neither makes his readers think, nor does he think himself what actual midmorning differences a heavy rain might have made or did actually make to the concrete actions and passions of the participants in the battle. He may refer truthfully enough to adverse conditions, but he does not even ask whether the soldiers cursed or sulked or laughed.

To say this is, I suggest, to say that for the unimaginative biographer the concepts that he perfectly, properly employs, concepts like 'heavy rain', 'severe casualties', and 'ammunition shortage' are concepts in which his mind rests. They are good beaten track concepts along which his intellectual feet are content to take their wonted and quite indispensable drill paces; whereas for the imaginative biographer who perfectly properly employs these very same concepts, they serve also as spring boards. *Because* he has found in the records that the rain was heavy or that the ammunition was running short, he wonders about the hungry riflemen's rations, and he wonders about the belatedness of the mules and pack-horses – and wondering he looks for evidence in the soldiers' letters, say, for comments on the state of their mid-day rations or of the depth of the mud in the Belgian road. To change the metaphor, instead of treating the concepts of 'heavy rain' and 'ammunition shortage' as cheques to be banked, he treats them as coins and notes that are meant to be exchanged here and now for consumable commodities. For him a conceptual cheque is something to make a lot of live purchases with. For his unimaginative confrère it was just an item in his financial holding; he did operate *with* it but he did not operate *from* it. He was not interested in its promises. He was not inclined to go on from ammunition shortage to pack-horses foundering in Belgium mud, or from ammunition shortage to a lowering of morale.

Let me illustrate the same point in another way. A man and a child come across a plank of wood by the roadside. The man just notices it, recognizes it for a plank, wonders for a moment who dropped it – and maybe, if a day or two later he needs a plank, he remembers its existence and goes to fetch it, in order to put it to one of its regulation plank-functions – repairing a crack in the poultry run, perhaps.

The child on the other hand, knowing quite well that it is only a plank, brings it home, where in one game it is a bridge, in the next it is a boat, and then an aeroplane, a battering ram and then a drum. When I say that it is these things, one after another, I mean that he treats it as such, and so operates with it, in one game after another. He sits on it and goes through the motions of rowing, or he straddles it across two chairs and trundles a cotton reel – I mean a steam roller – over it, and so on. The mere plank sets him off into one game after another. On seeing the plank he does not plan what things he will do with it. It, so to speak, releases his inventions of things to do with it. For the man there had just been a few fore-known and fore-knowable regulation-actions to perform with the plank; for the child there are no settled regulation things to do with it, but a limitless variety of non-pre-envisaged things that may occur to him to do with it.

Well, in partly the same way, the report of 'ammunition shortage' was a mere serviceable plank for the unimaginative biographer; for the imaginative one it was this and also a springboard for a limitless variety of non-pre-envisaged things that occurred to him to search for and to describe.

But, of course, the child is only playing, where the imaginative biographer is not playing but working. For the biographer has a many sided task – he has to collect and collate all the available evidence; he has to coordinate against a fixed time chart the movements of the various battalions and squadrons on both sides; he has to write up his story in a way easy to follow and within a roughly prescribed number of pages. His imaginative powers have to be in the service of, or at least in close partnership with, his powers as a ferreter-out of facts, as a statistician, as a book composer, and as many other things as well. The child has no such competing or cooperating calls upon him. He is just playing.

So to reduce this gap between imaginative playing and imaginative working, let us suppose that the child's mother gives him an otherwise dull job to do with the plank, maybe to close up the gap in the poultry-run. The child obediently does the dull job – and makes a game of it by treating the chickens as lions and tigers, the poultry-run as the jungle, and the plank as a thorn-zareba to keep the wild beasts out of the explorers' encampment. He now combines a necessary job of work with a game – what he may do with his thorn-zareba is now restricted by what he has been told to do about the gap in the chicken-run. He is now not just playing. He is more nearly in parallel with the imaginative biographer who may not just dream up the concrete detail of the ammunition shortage. He must marry what he dreams up with what the documentary evidence tells him. He may and should be imaginative, but he must not be fanciful. He must not just play. He must do a routine job of work, but he need not *just* do a routine job of work. He has to do what is necessary, but he may also do what is optional, or promising or intriguing, and so on.

This brings me to the last point that I want to make. I said much earlier that we are all tempted to mark off imagination from thought by confining imagination to the realm of fiction, as if to use one's imagination were *ipso facto* to indulge in make-believe. Instead I have been trying to satisfy you that a man's imaginativeness shows itself in any of those moments of his thinking in which he innovates, when he invents, discovers, explores, essays, experiments, and so on, that is when he makes or attempts to make moves which are new in the sense of being undrilled, unrehearsed and (for him) unprecedented, – for example making a new joke.

But now I want to consider why we are so apt to limit imagination to make-believers or to romancing.

Part of the reason, I suggest, is this. In comparing my two biographers of Napoleon, I described both of them as efficient fact-collectors and fact-collators; both of them as careful over their chronologies, topographies, statistics, and so on. But the second did better than the first in being imaginative as well.

That is, the biographical job was a complex of intellectual jobs. We had to give the two biographers their alphas, betas and gammas for a variety of different though interconnected intellectual attainments, of which imaginativeness was only one.

In contrast, the first activity of our child with the plank was not a consortium of cooperating activities. He had nothing that he was bound or expected to accomplish. He was just playing.

Rather similarly the novelist is emancipated from some of the obligations of the historian. He has not got to use evidence, and he has not got to displace or correct any rival narrative. We can discuss the merits of his story just *qua* a story, and not *qua* the alleged truth about any people or places. Mention of the novelist's deficiencies as a statistician, as a collator of manuscripts, or as a Sherlock Holmes would not come into our assessment of him *as a novelist*. It is not that his imagination is a faculty working on its own and by itself, but that the thinking that he does is and is intentionally exempted from a lot of the kinds of tasks which our thinking is usually jointly engaged in.

The painter who paints an imaginery portrait has to use all the skills and techniques that he uses when painting the portrait of a real live sitter – but he has exempted himself from the portrait-painter's special obligation to produce a likeness of Oliver Cromwell, say, or the Lord Mayor of London. Correspondingly our assessment of his picture is now *minus* any mention of its success or failure as a likeness of Cromwell or the Lord Mayor, since it is not trying to be a likeness. But this fact, that it is only a make-believe portrait does not entail that its artistry is higher in quality than that of a well-painted portrait. It may be flat and dead, where the portrait of the Lord Mayor was alive and 'speaking'. Imagination exercised in make-believe may be of a lower order than imagination exercised in history or portraiture. Edison's imaginative powers exceeded those of many writers of science fiction.

It is quite proper to say that *Pickwick Papers* is a work of imagination. But to say this is not to say that it is a work issued by a sub-department of Charles Dickens. More nearly, it is to say that it is a story which is *not* a history, *not* a scientific theory, *not* a coroner's report, *not* a piece of sociology, *not* a judge's summing-up, and so on. It does not try to do what these other things try to do, and so is exempt from the bad or good marks that it would merit if it did try to do them. Imagining is not something separate from thinking; but we can perform some thinking tasks without performing some others. We can give ourselves half-holidays. Make-believe is thought on a half-holiday from the tasks of advancing knowledge, or, what is different, from advancing plans or policies. But imaginativeness is not *more* of a necessity for make-believe than it is for advancing knowledge, or winning a campaign, or writing a history. I am not, of course, saying that Dickens' thinking, in being exempt from the requirements of evidence, chronological data, geographical latitudes and longitudes, etc., is as free and aimless as the wind. Novels, even if pure fairy-stories, are subject to a variety of canons, the flouting of which makes them bad or contemptible novels or fairy-stories. A half-holiday from certain specified obligations is not a half-holiday from all obligations. There are certain freedoms indulged in by Dickens or Hans Andersen which Jane Austen and Conrad do not allow themselves, and vise versa. But I do not want to discuss the variegated criteria between good and bad in the various genera and species of fiction. All I am trying to do here is to explain why we are tempted erroneously to assimilate imagining to make-believe, by the fact that pure make-believe is *ex officio* exempted from a lot of the chores to the performance of which imagination is only one ancillary amongst others. That is why we can call it 'pure' make-believe.

In summary, imagining is, I am maintaining, not an activity to be contrasted with thinking; nor yet a species of thinking. It is the innovating, inventing, exploring, adventuring risk-taking – if you like, creative, vanguard or scout-patrol – of thinking. That is why it has no place in those few highly mechanized branches of thinking in which our movements are treadmill-movements, as are the steps we take in computing. The thinker, in any field whatsoever, who knowingly ventures off or beyond the beaten track, is showing some degree of imaginativeness. His ventures may be and often are fruitless, random, cranky or crazy; or they may be and sometimes are fertile, coordinated, and shrewed. Except on the barrack-squares of life, the epithet 'unimaginative' is always somewhat disparaging. But while the epithets 'adventurous', 'inventive', and 'exploratory' are terms of praise, the epithets 'fanciful', 'reckless' and 'crazy' are terms of abuse.

Dreamers of dreams may be pathfinders; but they may be mere vagrants; and of those who depart from the pavements, only a few are explorers; the rest are mere jay-walkers.

I stress this depressing point just because there is a current sentimentalism which is tending to glorify the notion of imagination with a halo. People are beginning to boast of their imagination, as if there was no chance of a lively imagination being a silly one. Scope for originality is also scope for silliness. The genius is an imaginative thinker – but so is the crank. Sir Isaac Newton was both at once.

4

THINKING AND SELF-TEACHING

We are not often enough or deeply enough puzzled by the notions of thinking, pondering, reflecting, and the like, namely of what Rodin's *Le Penseur* looks as if he is absorbed in. I am not concerned with the dreamy notion of 'thinking=believing', which anyhow has been sadly overworked, usually in the wrong harness.

What is *Le Penseur* doing, seemingly in his Cartesian insides? Or, to sound scientific, what are the mental processes like, which are going on in that Cartesian *camera obscura*? We are, since we have to be, absolutely familiar with the *thing*, that is, with the cogitative doing or the process of pondering itself, for it has been at least off and on since our infancy, part of the pulse of our own existence. *Cogitamus ergo Sumus.* Yet we cannot, apparently, answer the simplest concrete questions about it. Why can't we? How could it, of all things, be hidden from us?

Notoriously some of our ponderings, but not all, terminate in the solutions of our problems; we had been fogged, but at last we came out into the clear. But if sometimes successful, why not always? If belatedly, why not promptly? If with difficulty, why not easily? Why indeed does it ever work? How possibly can it work? Notoriously, too, some people are better thinkers than others; and we ourselves may be better at thinking out the solutions of anagrams than at thinking out the solutions of chess-problems. Whence these disparities? What sort of an unevenly distributed craft or skill is this? Why did I acquire my own personal ration of it, and not yours instead? Why does not Mozart, indeed why cannot he, suddenly start thinking Immanuel Kant's thoughts, and vice versa? Why do not schools provide classes in thinking, as they do in mundane crafts like drawing, Latin, carpentry, and rifle-shooting? Ridiculous suggestion? Certainly. But then what makes it ridiculous to suggest that thinking is one teachable skill among others? Surely not anything like what would make it ridiculous to suggest that the natural processes of digesting and perspiring are extra skills that could and should be taught in schools or universities.

Let us pause a bit with this little riddle. Why would it be absurd for a school or university to offer a separate course of instruction in thinking? These are two reasons, one important but dull; the other important and interesting.

(1) The housewife who has separate shelves, hooks, containers, and bags marked flour, sugar, onions, mustard, etc., does not also have separate receptacles marked 'food', 'edibles', 'comestibles', or 'victuals', for the simple reason that she has already provided receptacles for all the species of these genera. Well, similarly, the school or college curriculum which promises courses in arithmetic, French grammar, Hittite archaeology, verse composition, etc., is already promising instruction in *species* of thinking. A student who has been taught some arithemetic or some French grammar has already learned in some measure to think out arithmetic problems or problems in composing or construing French prose. All learning is learning to tackle problems of this, that, or the other specific varieties. There are no residual problems of purely generic sorts.

(2) If the school or college promised to teach Originality, Invention, Wit, Pertinence, Initiative, Enterprise, Spontaneity, Talent, and Genius, we should feel sceptical. The lessons, exercises, tests competitions, etc., might indeed and should equip and encourage the students to attempt moves of their own, to compose sonnets or plays of their own, to design experiments of their own, and so on. But all these adventures, diminutive, modest, or striking, must be spontaneous, else they will not be essays, inventions, or compositions of the student's own. For it is to be *his* failure or *his* success, *his* good shot or *his* poor shot, it has *not* to be something contributed by the teacher. If it is the student's own sonnet, then it is not the teacher's sonnet, for all that the student would never have composed it without the teacher's suggestions, criticisms, and drills. Now the notion of thinking *is* the notion of thinking for oneself, of making one's own try, however perfunctory and diffident, at some problem, task, or difficulty. His instructors will have equipped and perhaps encouraged him to make his shot; but the shot is

his and not his instructors'. My initiatives, small or great, unsuccessful or successful, cannot, in logic, *be* what my teachers or my textbook did for me.

To keep our restricted deck-space fairly clear for the present I am going to leave on one side such off-centre things as the thinking of the man who is glumly brooding over an insult; the thinking of a man who is, for pleasure, running over in his head a tune or a poem that he has long since got by heart; and the thinking of the man who is just dreaming. We shall be concentrating on the man who is trying to think something out, whose thinking, unlike that of those others, can be successful or unsuccessful, bright or dull, industrious or idle, expert or amateurish, laborious or easy.

I am going to approach my objective by a knight's move, one which I think may surprise you a bit. For I am going to begin by reminding you of some truisms about teaching and therefore, necessarily, also about learning. Why? Because, to put it infantiley, my hope is to define thinking indirectly in terms of teaching. I am going to argue that *Le Penseur* is not, of course, engaged in privily teaching himself whatever it is that he wants to know – he cannot teach it because he does not know it – but that he is experimentally plying himself with might-be cues, clues, reminders, snubs, exercises, spurs, and the like, of types that are sometimes or often employed unexperimentally by teachers who are teaching what they do know. But we have some ground to cover first. Anyhow from the outset it seems plausible to say that *Le Penseur* could always have been saved from his present labours of pondering by getting someone else – the Angel Gabriel, say – to teach him the answer. So there is this connection between thinking and teaching. Thinking is trying to make up for a gap in one's education.

I am going to assume, what has been argued elsewhere, that, with a reservation or two, all teaching is teaching-*to* and all learning is learning-*to*. Even the memorizing of rhymes, dates and tunes qualifies as learning just in so far as it leads to more than mechanical echoing. The child has not begun to learn to spell who can recite, parrot-like, the dictated spellings 'C-A-T' CAT, and 'B-O-B' BOB. Only when he has begun to try to think up the right spellings or at least possible spellings for words to which he has not been alphabetically introduced, has he begun to learn to spell. To have learned to solve anagrams is to have

learned to solve new anagrams, not to play back the solutions of
anagrams already solved by the instructor. Later I am going to
lean heavily on these notions of teaching-*to* and being taught-*to*.
But I warn you that here I am flying in the faces of most N.C.O.'s
and of too many educationalists, who never doubt that teaching
consists in dictating things for subsequent verbatim
regurgitation. Naturally, though horrifying, some of them think
well of the potential teaching-utility of subliminal gramophones.
Tape recorders play back, but they do not learn. People who do
learn do not just play back. Even to have learned something by
heart is to have become able to do more than to parrot the piece. It
is to be able to detect and correct erroneous recitations, to recite
the piece and not some other piece when required to do so; to be
able to deliver it fast or slowly, to start it or stop it at required
places and so on.

Partly for ulterior reasons, but partly to dispel your
attachment, if it exists, to this superstition that learners are mere
players-back, I now remind you of a few of the
teaching-methods, devices, and dodges by which ordinarily
good or very good teachers do actually teach things to us.

(1) They tell us lots of things, of course, but with variations in
vocabulary, context, emphasis, and so on, sometimes *viva voce*
and sometimes in writing; with or without new illustrations,
expansions, elucidations, corollaries, etc. They do not repeat
themselves like cuckoo-clocks, or not much – and for obviously
good pedagogic reasons.

(2) They test us hardly at all for our ability to parrot their actual
words or to ape their actual movements, but for our ability and
readiness to exploit the lesson itself by applying it, re-phrasing
it, accelerating it, drawing conclusions from it, marrying it with
earlier lessons and the like; in short, by doing things on our own
with it.

(3) They teach us cricket-strokes, perspective-drawing and
French pronunciation, not much by describing anything, but by
showing us how the thing should and also how it should not be
done, and then getting us to move or utter, and *not* to move or
utter in similar ways.

(4) They tease us, like Socrates, with questions, and then with
further questions about our answers, and it is we who do the
answering.

(5) They make us practise and re-practise our five-finger

exercises and our conversions of syllogisms, with variations in tempo, syllogism-topic, etc.

(6) They lead us by the hand along a half-familiar track and leave us in the lurch to get ourselves over its final stretch.

(7) They cite or exhibit blatantly erroneous or inadequate solutions so that we, in recoil, improve them and/or pinpoint what was wrong in them; and they caricature our own sillier attempts in order to get us to ridicule them for ourselves.

(8) They draw our attention to partly analogous, but easier problems, and leave us to use these analogies as banisters.

(9) They break up complex problems into simpler ingredients and leave us to solve these unalarming ingredient problems, and then to reunite their solutions.

(10) When we have hit on the (or a) solution, they set us subsidiary or parallel problems in order to get us to consolidate and limber up our mastery of the original solution.

All of these and scores or hundreds of similar didactic moves, expedients, tactics, and dodges are intended by our teachers to get us ourselves to do and to say things of our own (as well as very often to undo and unsay things); for example, not just to parrot the recited spellings of a few given words but to attempt the spelling of hitherto unattempted words on the lines of those dictated specimens, and to withdraw or improve our first attempts.

Naturally and notoriously the pupil often fails to respond, or to respond well. He is, perhaps, scared, bored, sulky, stupid, restless, unambitious, or hostile, and the teacher is, perhaps, tired, shy, in a hurry, cross, pessimistic, and off his preferred subject. Conversely, the fact that the pupil has shown no sign of progress yesterday or today is quite compatible with his coming on fast next week or next term. Seeds often do germinate slowly. Muscles always are slow to harden up. Did you succeed in swimming in your first lesson? If not, had you learned nothing at all in that first lesson? I mention these truisms because *Le Penseur*'s own ponderings (which is what we are all along concerned with) can be in just the same plight. He, too, flogs away and makes no headway today; tomorrow he, too, seems to be in a worse muddle than ever; yet sometimes, though not always, for him, too, things will have sorted themselves out rather well after the weekend. Dividends often do arrive rather a long time after the investments are made. Thus the progress made or not made or not visibly made by *Le Penseur* resembles in several ways the progress made or not made or not visibly made by the teacher-pupil pair. Our question, 'Why does thinking not always work, or not always work quickly?' is in parallel with the same less puzzling questions about teaching.

Nonetheless, whatever their other similarities, *Le Penseur* is not himself, so to speak, a Siamese teacher-pupil pair. For the teacher knows the things that he tries to teach to his pupil; *Le Prenseur* is pondering just because he does not know what he wants to know. My thinking is not the instruction of pupil Gilbert by teacher Ryle. Gilbert Ryle, in his thinking, is trying to find out what no one, external or internal, is there to teach him. To ponder is to try to make up for *un*-instruction. What I am trying to think out for myself is indeed something that the Angel Gabriel conceivably might have known and taught me instead, but it is something that no one in fact did teach me. That is why I have to think. I swim because I am not a passenger on someone else's ferry-boat. I think, as I swim, for myself. No one else could do this for me.

Now I make a start on the second leg of my knight's move, namely to bring out a connection, *not* an identity, between being taught and thinking.

I have already declared that the pupil does not qualify as having even begun to spell or solve anagrams so long as all he is ready and able to do is to play back the dictated spellings of a few selected specimen words for the dictated solutions of a few specimen anagrams. Only when he begins to suggest possible spellings of his own for new words, or possible solutions of his own for new anagrams and to reject some such suggestions, does he qualify. Ditto for learning rock-climbing, chess, and philosophy. His blank repetition of what the teacher said or exhibited is not yet what the teacher was trying to get him to do. But notice now: when the pupil does make his own applications and misapplications in new tasks of what his teacher has told or exhibited, then he certainly qualifies as thinking. For he is now applying off his own bat a recently learned operation-pattern to a new subject or situation; he is today innovating according to a formerly set precedent; he is today chancing his arm subject to some previously inculcated safeguards. His frequent mistakes and failures are now his doing; his occasional successes are now his doing. It is he and not his teacher who now merits praise or blame for getting things right or wrong.

Here we are confronted by a seeming paradox. For we seem to be saying that in spelling or mispelling a new word, or in solving a new anagram, or in composing his own limerick or sonnet, the pupil is doing something on his own, which, therefore, he had not been taught. If it is his own sonnet or limerick, or his own anagram-solution, or his own spelling or misspelling of the word 'rabbit', then *that* could not have been something that his teacher had taught him. Conversely, if that sonnet, that anagram-solution, or that spelling of 'rabbit' had been taught by the teacher, then it was not the pupil who thought it up, but the teacher – or his teacher. However, the appearance of a paradox vanishes when we remember that having learned, say, to spell does not reduce to having become the passive recipient and subsequent automatic regurgitator of some dictated letter-sequences. It is to have become able and ready to attempt new applications of acquired patterns, methods, precedents and examples. The young rock-climber is first learning to climb when he ceases to tread *where* his teacher trod and begins to try to tread over new slopes *in the ways in which* his teacher treads.

I am not changing the subject when I now invite you to consider (A) what Socrates and the slave boy do in Plato's dialogue, the *Meno;* and (B) what they do in my sequel to that dialogue.

(A) Socrates asks the geometrically innocent slave boy how he would construct a square precisely double the area of a given square. In the end the boy comes out with the right answer, namely that the square on the diagonal of the original square is of twice the area of that square itself. But Socrates elicits this correct Pythagorean answer without *telling* the boy any geometrical truths, however simple. He merely asks him questions, and then by further questions gets him to abandon his first tempting answers. We need, for our purpose, to note a few points about this piece of interrogative pedagogics or tutorial cross-questioning.

(1) Though this point is not emphasized, the boy is already equipped with a modicum of elementary arithmetic and, of course, with colloquial Attic Greek.

(2) Unaided Socratic cross-questioning could not possibly have made similar progress or any progress at all towards the solution of factual questions about, say, the casualties at Marathon or the date of the next eclipse of the sun. Nor could *Le Penseur*'s unaided ponderings.

(3) Though Socrates draws his famous moral that the boy must in a previous existence have got to know that Pythagorean theorem for it to be able to be elicited from him be mere questioning, we, surely like all the disputatious young men in the Academy who were any good, flatly reject this moral on the obvious ground that if, without still ulterior memory-flogging, the boy had been able in that supposed previous existence to discover the Pythagorean theorem by thinking, then there is nothing to prevent the boy from discovering it by thinking today. How was it originally discovered? Some solutions to some problems are attainable by pondering; all the more so when the ponderer is cunningly and persistently barked at by a Socratic sheepdog who already knows the way.

(4) Although the boy has given to each question, one by one, first his ill-thought-out answers and finally the wanted well-thought-out answer, still he does not claim to have thought out the whole proof for himself. After a fumble or two he had picked up each of the several links one by one, but it was Socrates who had controlled the chain. Already knowing the proof of Pythagoras' Theorem, Socrates, unlike the boy and also unlike *Le Penseur*, knew all along what questions were the right questions to ask and what was the right, or at least a suitable, sequence in which to ask them.

(B) Now listen to my own fabrication, namely the story of Socrates' *second* interview with the boy. Socrates begins again by putting a theorem-sized question to the boy; and he starts off as before by posing appropriate questions and demolishing the boy's initial answers to them. But now – oh horror! – Socrates realizes that he himself has either quite forgotten or, even worse, never had mastered the second half of this second theorem's proof. He has no idea how to go on; and, as Euclid's *Elements* has not been published yet, he cannot even surreptitiously consult that will-be standard work. What is to be done? He frankly confesses the crisis to the boy, who, to start with, sees no difficulty. He says, 'But yesterday, Socrates, you did not tell me any of the answers; you only asked me questions, to which I myself after some false starts gave *you* the right answers. Why can't we do that again? You don't need to know their answers in order to ask questions.'

Socrates explains that randomly thrown out questions cannot be expected to assemble themselves into a proof-generating sequence, but he concedes that with huge luck they might do so; and he concedes that he, Socrates, has had enough teaching experience in general, and has enough geometrical knowledge in particular to avoid asking lunatic, irrelevant, or infantile questions and to see through grossly silly answers. He cannot, as yesterday, pilot the slave boy, since today he does not know the channels. But he can make and coordinate some conjectural pilot-like suggestions and experiments, and he can now and then spot where rocks and shoals might be before getting to them. He is at home on salt water in general, though not on this particular stretch of it.

So Socrates starts off, pessimistically enough, trying out a question that occurs to him and then another and another; and by lunchtime all the progress they have made is the negative discovery that most of these particular questions had better not be asked again; though one or two short question-sequences had felt a bit promising. And that, very likely, is all the progress that they do make. But it could be that on the next day Socrates and the boy are getting an idea of some of the deeps and shallows, some of the headlands and islands. Even if steering directly towards their unseen goal is still impossible, steering away from specific troubles is becoming fairly easy. Perhaps eventually Socrates' initially chartless quasi-piloting fetches them nearly or even exactly where they want to be. Explorers always do have to start off chartless; yet, as we know, some of them sometimes with luck, flair, patience, and an already trained eye for country, end up with a bit of what had been no-man's-land now properly charted.

Now for my moral. This joint plight of the slave boy and my Socrates who on this occasion had not done his geometrical homework is precisely the plight that Pythagoras himself had been in during the hours or weeks when he was still trying to discover a proof of his own dear Pythagoras' Theorem. For hours or weeks Pythagoras had been his own slave boy being plied by his own unprepared Socratic self with hesitantly mooted candidate-questions nearly, though not quite, randomly hit on, and tentatively posed in nearly, but not quite, random sequences. By thinking he eventually solved his problem without once during the entire course of his ponderings being yet equipped to teach himself or anyone else its solution. He had not, and no one had, done his homework. It was not yet there to do, as it has been there ever since.

Unlike the guide who leads his docile companions along paths that already exist and are already familiar to him, though not to them, the pioneering pathfinder, Pythagoras say, has no tracks to follow; and any particular sequence of paces that tentatively takes through the jungle may soon have to be marked by him as leading only into swamps or thickets. All the same, it may be, though it need not be, that in a day's time or a year's time he will have made a track along which he can now guide docile companions safely and easily right through the jungle. How does he achieve this? Not by following tracks, since there are none to follow. Not by sitting down and wringing his hands. But by walking over ground where tracks certainly do not exist, but where, with luck, assiduity, and judgment, tracks might and so perhaps *will* exist. All his walkings are experimental walkings on hypothetical tracks or candidate-tracks or could-be tracks, or tracks on appro; and it is by so walking that, in the end, while of course he finds lots and lots of impasses, he also finds (if he *does* find) a viable track.

Pythagoras or, in general, Le Penseur is also in just this same unencouraging position. Tracks are found by the pioneer (if they *are* found), only by quasi-following could-be tracks, that is, by his experimentally trying out on appro one bit of ground after another to see if they could henceforth be unanxiously trodden by docile travellers who are not exploring.

There is my moral. Let me stiffen it with two cautionary remarks:

(1) To repeat: Pythagoras in trying to think out the proof of his theorem is not teaching himself this proof, since he has not yet found it. Nor is my Socrates teaching the boy the thing that he has omitted to prepare himself with.

(2) Pythagoras, my Socrates or, to generalize, Le Penseur, is tentatively, experimentally, suspiciously, and quite likely despondently trying out on himself expedients, routines, procedures, exercises, curbs, and dodges of types which teachers do employ, not always successfully, when they want to

teach things that they know to pupils who do not. He is trying them out on himself to see if they will be effective, which very often they will not be. They are not already established leads to his goal, but only could-be leads or candidate-clues or potential clues, like the As-If tutorial questions unconfidently put to the slave boy by my geometrically unprepared Socrates.

To say that *Le Preseur* is experimentally subjecting himself to on appro tutorial questions, clues, deterrents, exercises and the like, is not to say merely that he is being histrionic. He need not be, though he may be, aping his old headmaster or his former geometry tutor. The expert moves that you make in climbing the cliff-face may be imitated by a mere mimic; but the patterns of them may also be applied experimentally by the young climber who is trying out ways of scrambling upwards on such cliff-faces. He is deliberately trying to climb cliffs after the ways in which you climb them. He is not aping you but learning to do things of sorts that you have long since learned to do. He is following your examples, not trying to simulate your motions. His success, if he does succeed, is a bit of scaling, not a bit of representing.

Naturally my *Penseur* knows what it is like to be taught things that he does not know by teachers who do; and he knows what it is or would be like himself to be the teacher of some things that he knows to others who do not. So now he experimentally applies to himself, just in case they may turn out to be effective, operations of types that are often or sometimes employed effectively by live teachers upon live pupils. He chalks upon the back of an envelope a diagram, which he does not know to be even an approximation to the right one, in the rather faint hope that it may get him to see something that he needs to see, in the way in which the right diagram on the classroom blackboard often but not always does get the students to see what they need to see. Or he suspiciously concocts for his still unfledged argument a candidate-premise just to see whether it will work, or can be modified into working, as a premise in his argument. It is not yet a premise. It is a premise on appro. He is not basing anything on it; he is only As-If basing something on it. He is not just theatrically staging the moves of an arguer; and he is not just playing at arguing; he is working, working experimentally with a merely could-be argument-step. This is what an hypothesis is: a could-be premise on appro.

We began with some vexatious teasers about thinking, like 'if it is an art, craft, or skill, how do we acquire it, and why do schools not give special instruction in it? Why does it not always work? How does it ever work?' Now we can see, just one rung lower down on the sophistication-ladder, that the same questions, though still vexatious, are not quite as vexatious when asked about teaching. Is teaching one art, craft, or skill among others? Could universities teach it? What would they be teaching you in just teaching you to teach (period)?

No, teaching, like thinking, is after all not just one art or skill among others, any more than cooking is one soufflé among others. Yet it remains true, though I think unimportantly true, that there do exist instructional dodges and expedients, varying with different pupils and with different kinds of lessons, without which a good golfer may be a poor golf coach; or without which a new Comprehensive School teacher of French may cope less effectively with her unruly charges than does her colleague whose French is much weaker. I suppose it is such crafts that Colleges of Education do teach. For 'education' is not itself the name of one teachable craft among others. 'Learning to teach . . .' is an unfinished phrase, because 'teaching . . .' is unfinished.

My concluding point is this. Plato said that in thinking the soul is conversing with herself; or maybe 'debating' would be nearer the Greek. J. B. Watson said that thinking is sub-*saying*; plenty of philosophers and psychologists declare that all thinking is conducted *in* symbols, or *in* words and sentences, or *in* pictures or *in* diagrams or *in* formulae, etc. The metaphor of words or sentences being the vehicles of thought has still a vogue, and the idea that thought, like American golfers, is in need of vehicles seems to be quite generally swallowed. But what sorts of generalizations about thinking are these? Have amateur or professional introspections revealed this general dependence of thinking upon wording? But if that is all, might not Trobrianders think well enough without such vehicles? After all, we Europeans do eat with knives, forks, and spoons. Yet Trobrianders, maybe, eat without gastronomic vehicles. Or are these generalizations about thinking supposed to be conceptual necessities? Yet if so, just how does the description of someone as, after breakfast, *pensant*, carry with it the information that during that time he was saying things to himself in his head or picturing things to himself in his mind's eye?

We can now cope with this bother in two moves:

(1) For person A to teach person B something, A must either say things to B, which B hears, takes in, etc.; or A writes things or draws things, which B reads, copies, takes in, etc.; or A demonstrates or shows things to B, which B sees or hears or tastes or smells, etc.; or A audibly jeers at B or visibly reckons or frowns to him, or noticeably pauses meaningfully; and so on and so on. A cannot teach B without communicating with him. Lessons have to be got across, often across a classroom. Lessons are a very special sub-species of interpersonal communications, namely of educatively intended communications. *Of course,* the tuition of B by A requires vehicles.

(2) So, in so far as *Le Penseur* is occupied in experimentally or on appro trying out on himself, as on his inner slave boy, things of the sorts that constitute the vehicles by which live teacher A conveys his lessons to live pupil B, he is necessarily operating, overtly or just in imagination, *with* and *on* such things as words, sentences, diagrams, signals, gestures, etc. He is not, as we have seen, just mimicking real teachers; but he, just as much as the actor who is mimicking Socrates or Mr. Chips, has in logic to do the sorts of things that are done by Socrates and Mr. Chips in teaching their pupils. We might parody Plato and say that in thinking the soul is not just conversing or debating with herself; she is experimentally conveying could-be lessons to herself. Sometimes she is quasi-lecturing to herself; old-style German thinkers seemed to be doing this all the time.

Cartesians love to depict the activity of the thinker as consisting of supremely immaterial ingredients, such impalpable ingredients as ideas, intuitions and insight. In fact, the crude stuff of thinking has to consist of the perfectly ordinary vehicles of everyday interpersonal lesson-communication, though here employed not in its normal didactic task, but in the parasitic or higher-order task of query-tuition. It does not matter whether *Le Penseur* actually draws his diagrams on paper, or visualizes them as so drawn; and it does not matter whether in his quasi-posing his on appro Socratic questions to himself he speaks these aloud, mutters them under his breath, or only As-If mutters them on his mind's tongue. What matters is what he is trying to do, and is sometimes succeeding in doing, by thus overtly or covertly plying himself with these candidate-lesson-vehicles; for example, that he is trying to find, and is sometimes finding, the proofs of theorems. As A's well-charted teaching can occasionally dispel B's ignorance, so my uncharted thinking can occasionally dispel my own ignorance. Thinking is trying to better one's instructions; it is trying out promising tracks which will exist, if they ever do exist, only after one has stumbled exploringly over ground where they are not.

5

THINKING AND SAYING

There have always existed in the breasts of philosophers, including our own breasts, two conflicting tempers. I nickname them the 'Reductionist' and the 'Duplicationist' tempers, or the 'Deflationary' and the 'Inflationary' tempers. The slogan of the first temper is 'Nothing But . . .'; that of the other 'Something Else as Well . . .'

I give five different illustrations:

(1) Men, it is commonly declared, have in them Nothing But what they share in different degrees with animals. In opposition it is commonly declared that men have in them Something Else as Well that animals have not got in them at all, Soul or Reason or Spirit or the Divine Spark.

(2) Animals, we all incline to think, have in them Nothing But what is material, physical, chemical, or mechanical. We all, however, incline instead to think that animals have an Additional Something in them, namely Life, Self-Motion, or Purposiveness, which machines, pendulums, and electrical discharges are without.

(3) A social and political community is surely nothing over and above the several individuals who belong to it. They are its brass tacks. But on the other hand surely there is in a society some uniting agency or principle superadded to its members – the enveloping fabric behind and beneath those brass tacks.

(4) A physical object, like a planet, pebble, or person, must reduce without residue to the sensations registered when an observer has sense-perception of it. Yet on the other hand there must exist in addition a substantial It or anyhow a substantial He to be the origin, the anchor or anyhow the recorder of these sensations.

(5) Lastly, the mind, as Hume tells us, just *is* the mutitudinous impressions, ideas, impulses, volitions, and feelings that

constitute the phosphorescent cascade of consciousness. But a Descartes tells us, instead, that the mind *is* that which owns, monitors, controls, remembers and forgets these snatches of cogitation. Or, to be up to date and tough, a person's mind is Nothing But the ways in which he visibly, palpably, and audibly behaves; unless our tender, anti-Behaviourist conscience is right to protest that his observable muscular movements and his audible utterances will be those of a Robot, unless they are the outward manifestations of a privately thinking, feeling, and willing Self or Ego.

The specific notion of Thinking, which is our long-term concern, has been duly deflated by some philosophers into Nothing But such and such; and duly reinflated by others into Something Else as Well. On the one view, *Le Penseur*'s thinking is just the working of a non-man-made computing machine; or else, on the contrary view, his Thinking is something special which could not without logical absurdity be credited to a mere machine.

But long before nearing my quarry and arguing that Reductionist and Duplicationist theories about thinking are the heads and tails sides of one and the same mistake, I am going to analyze three or four trumped-up and emotion-free specimens of head-on collisions between Reductionism and Duplicationism, hoping that we may identify, near home and on a small scale, the kind of road-surface on which a Hobbes and a Descartes, and Occam and a Plato skid into their opposite ditches.

Suppose that of two boys one is engaged in writing a homesick letter to his mother, the other in mimicking the letter-writer to amuse spectators. If the mimicry is faithful, the two boys do exactly the same things – otherwise the mimicry is not faithful. The ink marks made on his notepaper by the letter-writer are accurately repeated by the mimic on his notepaper. The frowns, grunts, and pen-dippings of the mimic are exact replicas of those of his victim. 'Since there was no witnessable difference, so,' now says our Reductionist, 'there was no difference of any sort between what the two boys were doing.' 'Nonsense!' says our Duplicationist. 'There was all the difference in the world, only it was a necessarily unwitnessable difference, between the activity of writing a homesick letter and that of entertaining spectators with a piece of malicious play-acting. Why else would you pick the one boy, but not the other, to act in your charades? Consequently, besides the scrawling, frowning, and pen-dipping that the mimic and the letter-writer were both seen doing, the mimic must have been doing some invisible Something Else as Well, namely his private and internal acts of *simulating*, which the letter-writer was not performing.' 'Rubbish!' rightly objects our Reductionist, 'What could these supposed private and internal acts of simulating, say, the dipping of a pen in the inkpot, be like, that he executes in his mental *camera obscura* where there is no pen or inkpot? And what would be the point of the mimic trying to entertain spectators by performing, invisibly to them, your postulated private and internal histrionic acts, which, you agree, anyhow were not performed by the letter-writer?'

Already we have found one cardinal negative thing. Rather surprisingly our Reductionist and our Duplicationist had agreed on one central point, namely in assuming that the mimic's lifelike histrionic actions could have differed from the actions of his victim only by his additional performing extra *actions* (or part-actions) that the other had not performed. Since no such extra actions were witnessed, therefore, on the one view, there was no difference of any sort between the boys' actions. And since there were differences between their actions, therefore, on the other view, the mimic must have performed some extra actions, but internal, unobserved ones. This central point on which they were agreed was the key point on which they were both wrong. Action A can, by accident or, as here, by design, be muscularly and photographically the perfect replica of action B, while conspicuously being a completely different sort of action. In our example two conspicuous differences between the boys' actions occur to us at once:

(1) The mimic scribbled with an entirely different *intention* from that of the letter-writer, with the intention, namely, of diverting the spectators by visibly doing just what the letter-writer was seen doing, who, for his part, intended only to lament to his mother. Hence the mimic, but not the letter-writer, would have stopped when the spectators lost interest.

(2) Moreover, in his simulations the mimic exercised *skills* that the other boy was not exercising. The spectators could see for themselves how well or badly he was play-acting. Intentions and skills are overlooked by the Reductionist since they are no

part of the photographable muscular movements to which he categorially mis-deflates actions. By the Duplicationist they are not ignored but they are categorially mis-inflated into extra, but nonmuscular Actions which, because Inner Actions, transcend the spectators' observations.

Consider some analogies:

(A) The ambassador signing a treaty makes pen-strikes exactly like those he had made after breakfast when trying out his pen nib on an old envelope. Yet by the one bit of penmanship, and not by the other, he commits his country to an alliance or a surrender. For he inscribes his signature (1) on the treaty-document (and not on an old envelope); (2) in his capacity as accredited representative of his country's government; (3) after consultation with his Foreign Office; (4) in the Chamber and at the time officially appointed; (5) not under duress; (6) in the presence of his co-signatories; (7) not in the dark; (8) with the accompaniment of certain ceremonies, and so on.

Such conditions as these make his action the politically important action that it is without, *per impossibile*, being additional actions that he is performing. They do qualify his actions, but not by qualifications that could be expressed by simple active verbs or simple adjectives, Hobbist or Cartesian, Carnapian or Hegelian, to which his name would be nominative. They provide what he does with its point, its credentials, and its force. But they import neither visible nor invisible differences into his penmanship.

(B) Whether the player scored a goal when he kicked the ball between the goalposts depends on many things. Was he offside? Was it during an interval? Was the game itself a game of Hockey or Polo? Were the goalposts those of his own side? Had the ball or the player strayed in from an adjacent game? Was the ball a ping-pong ball? and so on. Scoring a goal is neither to be deflated into just kicking a ball between some posts nor inflated into kicking a ball and performing an additional, though private and nonmuscular action of scoring as well. It is kicking a ball between posts when several complex antecedent and collateral conditions are satisfied – the satisfaction or non-satisfaction of which, incidentally, is ordinarily perfectly obvious to the unmetaphysical referee. Notice, *en passant*, that the stating of these very familiar conditions is going to require quite a chapter of subordinate clauses, beginning 'When . . .', 'Unless . . .', 'Provided that . . .', 'Where . . .', etc.

(C) Until the English law was changed, housebreaking differed from burglary only in the time of day at which it was committed. So the felon whose watch was unreliable might totally mistake the legal nature of his very own felonious act; introspection could not help him.

(D) The novice, whose move with his Queen has put his opponent's King in check, may recollect doing nothing else than moving his Queen. He had indeed made no additional move, but this one move he did make, with the pieces disposed on the board as they were and the rules of chess being what they are, had had a chess-consequence which he had not planned and did not perceive. The statement of what it is for a King to be put in check would have a fairly complicated syntax. A King, on being put into check, does not alter in colour, shape, size, weight, or position. Is getting into check, then, an unverifiable alteration? But what could be more conclusively verified than that a King is, or else is not, in check? Unobservable? Nonsense! Photographable? Well, in a solitary snapshot of him by himself, no. But in a sequence of photos of the whole board, and all its occupants, in their several successive positions, certainly yes.

Before leaving these mini-hurdles that I have set up in order revealingly to catch the feet of our Reductionist and Duplicationist, we should develop a point of epistemology that has so far been left in the background. Our Reductionist is *ex officio* a zealous empiricist, whose constant complaint is that his Platonic or Cartesian or Hegelian opponent always fetches in unverifiables or unobservables to provide him with his occupational Something Else as Well. We sympathize until we find that our empiricist's own roster of observables is becoming disturbingly short, and his roster of unobservables disturbingly long. It appears that 'strictly' the referee cannot *see* that the player, *qua* not being offside, has scored a goal, for a sharper-eyed Red Indian sees well the flight of the ball and the player's muscular movements, but, in his ignorance of the rules of football, sees not at all that, since the player is not offside, he has scored a goal. How possibly then can the referee, with his inferior eyesight, 'strictly' see what the Red Indian cannot see?

We are told, to our surprise, that what is 'Strictly' observed is what could not be mistaken, requires no special schooling, incorporates no estimates, allowances, or inferences, and rests on no arguments. Hence the sergeant cannot 'strictly' observe that the recruit is *obeying* his order to present arms, but only that he is presenting arms the moment after being ordered to do so; and spectators cannot 'strictly' observe differences between the mimic's and the letter-writer's actions, or between those of the ambassador in signing a treaty and in testing his pen nib. Nor can the illiterate 'strictly' see a misprint. Nor, presumably, can the astronomer 'strictly' observe the moon being eclipsed.

Our Reductionist had begun by assailing Cartesian and Platonic extravagances on the basis of what can be, in an ordinary way, observed. But now he reduces, in its turn, observation itself to Nothing But some oddly stingy minimum. He deflates his own deflator.

However, this stinginess of the empiricist must not soften us towards the lavishness of the transcendentalist. For though he properly acknowledges the differences between kicking and scoring, or between just presenting arms and obeying the order to present arms, yet he goes on to make these differences occult ones. For since they are not to be the earthly or muscular differences demanded in vain by the empiricist, they will have instead to be unearthly, nonmuscular differences that transcend the referee's and the sergeant's powers of perception.

Let us, however, without debating them, leave behind us these theories of knowledge.

Now, at rather long last, we can advance beyond our contrived stalking horses to punish the categorial maltreatments given by our Platonizers no less than by our Occamizers to that special notion of *thinking* which is our real concern. This notion of thinking is that of pondering or trying to solve a problem, not that of believing or feeling sure, which unfortunately goes by the same English name of 'Thinking'. I am interested in cogitation, not credence; in perplexity, not unperplexity. Our specimen thinker is going to be the still baffled *Penseur*, not the man who, having reached conviction, has stopped struggling to reach it.

I shall very cursorily just remind you, before jettisoning it, of that old fairy-story about thinking that was the stock-in-trade of, among others, Descartes, Locke, Berkeley, Hume, Hartley, Reid, John Stuart Mill, and even Virginia Woolf – I mean the psychological fable about the introspectible ingredients of our private streams of consciousness, namely, the famous 'simple ideas', those dim traces and faint echoes of bygone impressions, the coagulations of these ideas into complex and fictional ideas, the couplings of them into true or false judgments, the distillations out of them of abstract ideas, and their inferential leap-froggings. If we did not know, we could now guess that there would have to arise a Hume to 'reduce' thinking to mere processions of these faint and derivative introspectibles down channels shallowly dug by Association; and how there would then have to arise a Kant or a Bradley to impose upon these processions some responsible controls that transcend the pryings of introspection.

Instead I shall concentrate on a contemporary substitute for this introspectionist fable. It is a genuine, though only a partial improvement on its now friendless Lockean or Humean predecessor. One of its slogans, a portentous and predominantly silly one, is 'Thought is Language', a slogan which I expect you have met and I hope you have winced at. However there are two meritorious points that are sometimes intended by the silly slogan, namely:

(A) Whatever we think of the alleged private ingredients of our Humean streams of consciousness, at least we have to acknowledge that what a person concludes, surmises, calculates, proves, objects, decides, or forecasts must be something stated or statable in a public language. An unworded proof is no more a proof than an unworded poem is a poem, an unformulated verdict is a verdict, or unworded repartee is repartee. The result at which a thinker arrives (if he does arrive), is in some important classes of cases a printable truth or falsehood, e.g. an equation, an allegation, a theorem, or an hypothesis. (It is often overlooked that even to this generalization there are plenty of exceptions. A Mozart's thinking results in something playable, not statable. A symphony is not composed in English or German, it has no translation, there is no evidence for or against it. It is not grammatical or ungrammatical; neither in prose nor in verse. A Cezanne may make mistakes, but he is not in error. There is no contradicting the chessplayer's carefully or carelessly thought-out move. A sonnet is not a report, a premise, or a conclusion; it can be a bad sonnet, but it cannot be a fallacious one.)

It is, then an important improvement on the Locke-Hume fable, that we do now rightly insist that the products of at least some thinking are such things as published or publishable truths or falsehoods, and no longer only unsharable introspectibles. One place in which to look for the products of some thinking is a public library. I am going, for this occasion, to restrict myself to such thinkings as do result, if at all, in such things as worded propositions, since my subject is 'Thinking and Saying'.

(B) A quite different and independent thing that is often intended by the silly slogan 'Thought is Language' is this. It is declared with partial, but only partial truth, that in the pondering that *Le Penseur* is still engaged in before he solves or abandons his problem, he must be inwardly conducting, however intermittently and fragmentarily, worded monologues; he must be soliloquizing in his head or *sotto voce*. According to some 'All Thinking is Thinking in Symbols', 'Thinking is Talking to Oneself', or even 'Thinking is Nothing But Saying Things to Oneself'. (This partially correct point also must not be universalized. If Mozart and Cezanne verbally soliloquize at all at their work, this cannot be part of their composing.)

Anyhow here, at last, we reach the two places on the road where occur all those skids into the vulgar Occamist ditch on the left, as well as all those skids into the genteel Platonist ditch on the right.

(A) Our Duplicationist argues, with initial correctness, that the thinker's result, when of the propositional kind, is not merely a string of words linked in a grammatically tolerable sentence, since his proof of the theorem, say, or his analysis of the general's strategy is a contribution to geometry or to military history, not just to French or Russian prose. What he has found is, say, a new truth and not just a new locution, and a truth which is carried equally well by its original French and by its subsequent Spanish wordings. So the new geometrical or historical truth, say, that he has thought out *is* not just one of these many alternative locutions; it is their unitary burthen or their objective, communicable Meaning. Bits of language may be necessary, but only as the interpersonal vehicles of objective Meanings that are thinkable, in principle, to any hearers or readers of any nationalities.

At this point, of course, our Quine-like Reductionist rudely asks what these Meanings are like, what they are made of, how they differ from the Lockean ideas that they had so promisingly replaced, and especially how you and I can decide whether we are crediting the same sentences with the same or even with similar Meanings. For example with the same or even with similar truth-cargoes.

(B) Correspondingly, when our Duplicationist moves on to consider, no longer the statable products, but the processes and toils of *Le Penseur*'s ponderings while he is still short of his goal, he unsuspiciously accepts these sweeping equations, 'Thinking is Talking to Oneself in one's head' and 'All Thinking is Thinking in bits of Language', though of course with his inevitable supplementation that *Le Penseur*'s thinking *is* not that deploying to himself in his head the words, phrases and sentences that he admittedly does; it *is*, rather , his cogitatively deploying, in orderly or disorderly processions, the objective, communicable Meanings of those soliloquized words, phrases, and sentences. These Meanings are for the Duplicationist those significance-cargoes that are carried indifferently by your French and my English internal locutions – though the challenge to exhibit to his Reductionist critic even one such cargo, prised off its French or English vehicle, is as usual unwelcome to him.

Well then, what do *we* do? We begin by jettisoning the vehicle-cargo model. A comprehended locution does indeed differ from that locution heard but uncomprehended; but not by being a couple of things apprehended. A thing said with a point and for its point does indeed differ from that thing said in delirium or by rote, but not by being a couple of things said. In owing a penny I am indeed, despite the reductionist, richer than when I own a mere metal disc. Unlike the mere metal disc, my penny has some purchasing power. Yet, despite the Duplicationist, owning a disc with purchasing power is not owning two articles, a metal vehicle and also a non-metallic, unpocketable yet marketable cargo. In owning a penny I own a disc with which I am empowered by laws, regulations, conventions, market-practices, etc., to buy, rent, lend, tip, invest, repay, give change, etc., if and, roughly, whenever I choose. It is an institutionally qualified *enabling*-instrument. It is a disc that I can *use* in quite specific ways. It is not a disc *and* something else as well; and it is not just a disc; it is a disc that is completely qualified for some quite specific sorts of transactions. The formulation of these qualifications would require not just some simple auxiliary nouns, simple adjectives, or simple verbs but a whole batch of syntactically variegated subordinate clauses. Imagine the shape that would be taken by your explanation to a schoolboy of how his Victorian shilling-piece has lost its purchasing power; or even by your explanation of what it is that it has lost.

In much the same way a word and its meaning are not two things that I acquire when I learn the word, for all that learning its meaning certainly is learning more than its pronounciation and spelling. I, in learning its meaning, am becoming more or less lastingly enabled to conduct with it, if and, roughly, whenever I choose, hosts of, *inter alia*, informative, calculative, recording, anagram-solving, and versifying transactions of quite specific kinds. The word is not a noise *and* something else as well; and it is not just a noise. It is a complexly qualified noise, a noise endowed with a quite specific *saying*-power, endowed sometimes by institutional regulations, generally by accumulating public custom, slightly rigorized by pedagogic disciplines; and so on. It is a semi-institutional *enabling*-instrument. It is something that we have learned how to use and how not to misuse.

If Tweedledum now characteristically grumbles that we cannot 'strictly' see in the black marks on the printed page, or 'strictly' hear in the syllables of the lecturer anything that demarcates a jumble of letters of the alphabet from a word, a jumble of syllables from a phrase, or, to generalize, what conveys from what does not convey a sense or one such meaning from another, we, remembering our referee and our Red Indian, can unanxiously reply as follows: 'The very person who both can and does in daily life, with a few, but only a few errors, confusions, or hesitations, make these disallowed discriminations of yours is just the ordinary reader or listener, like yourself (or in special cases, the expert reader or listener),

who reads with his quite ordinary eyes the printed marks, or
listens with his quite ordinary ears to the spoken syllables, given
only that, like our referee, and unlike our Red Indian, his wits
have been suitably trained and that he is here and now
exercising these wits. You, having learned how, are now
availing yourself of the printed marks or the spoken syllables, in
your talking and your writing to others. Just so, too, you, in
talking to yourself in your head, as well as in talking to me aloud
(unless you are just babbling deliriously), are here and now
making actual use of words and phrases, grammatical
constructions, etc., the mastery of which you have retained since
you acquired it.'

But making *what* use? Precisely how is the still baffled
Pythagoras *employing* the things that he is saying in his head or
muttering *sotto voce*? This is our special crux. For making an
entry in a diary is doing a very different kind of employing from
reminding a colleague of a meeting, from ordering a taxi, from
telling an anecdote, from cursing, or from wilfully giving to the
public a piece of misinformation. Our purposes in asking
questions differ from our purposes in praying, scolding,
play-acting, multiplying, and will-drafting. Sometimes
philosophers speak as if behind all or most of our sayings there
is the monolithic intention to induce beliefs in our interlocutor.
But there is no such uniform intention. Sometimes we mean to
amuse, reassure, or scandalize him, or to evoke sympathy from
him; or to reprimand him; and sometimes it is to ourselves, and
not to an interlocutor that we say things, and so on, and so on.
But our special question is now this fairly definite one: With
what *particular* intention or intentions, then, does Pythagoras
'say' the particular things that he 'says to himself' during those
periods when he is tackling a still baffling problem? What is the
point of the under-breath muttering which the thinker really is
very often doing when thinking? What is the heuristic *use* of
soliloquizing? There is no one-strand answer. The still baffled
Pythagoras, in again and again muttering a geometrical phrase
to himself, may be intending, by way of rehearsal, to fix it in his
memory; or in discontent with its slack phrasing, he may be
intending, if he can, to stiffen it; or he may be meaning to
re-savour the thrill of a recent discovery; or he may be muttering
with no intention at all, but involuntarily, like the jingles that
run remorselessly in our heads. Yet a dictaphone recording of

his mutterings might easily fail to betray which of these or other needs or automatisms explains the mutterings.

But we can do better than merely remind ourselves of these innumerable possible soliloquizing-intentions. A person who is trying to puzzle out by himself the solution to a problem, an anagram, perhaps, or a philosophical crux, or a statesman's tangle, is, as Plato saw, plying himself with most of the same things as those that two people ply each other with when they are interestedly discussing with one another a problem of which neither has the solution. So let us consider some of the particular, easily avowable intentions with which you and I ordinarily say the things we say to each other in our live discussions. Neither of us is equipped didactically to impart to his companion bits of that wanted solution, corollaries of it, or premises from which it follows. Discussing is not telling and telling is not discussing. So what can be the heuristic use or point of the undogmatic things said by us in our discussion? What do we recognize as rendering this or that contribution to our discussion successful or unsuccessful? As we know, discussions do, sometimes, get issues settled or partly settled. Though neither of us participants can pilot the other or himself, yet between us we may (though also we may not), make steady or erratic, great or slight progress towards our hidden goal. But how possibly *can* things that we say to each other in ignorance or perplexity mend that ignorance or allay that perplexity?

Well, one answer is this: we can say things *experimentally* to each other. Experiments do not necessarily succeed, but they do not necessarily fail. A, without any conviction, makes to B a tentative suggestion that is new to B, and this may (but of course may not) provoke an impromptu response from him, which in turn may elicit from A a new objection, a new parallel, or a new follow-up; and this may promise, perhaps falsely but perhaps truly, to prove fertile before long. Or B smells something funny in a thing impatiently blurted out by A, who in his turn, now finds a trace of the same ridiculousness in a point that they had both hitherto taken solemnly. Or B flippantly half-draws from a hint hesitantly made by A a possible consequence which suddenly looks like tying in surprisingly neatly with a recently shelved surmise. Or A, having nothing to reply, frowns or wriggles and so may induce in B an uncomplacency which may, but need not, make him seek a previously unthought-of safeguard, or try a previously neglected evasive action. Or B, bankrupt of ideas, tries just putting into different words points of which both are getting tired, in the hope, sometimes realized, that the fresh wording will suggest new developments, examples, or hazards. And so on.

My focal point is this. The things that A and B say to each other, together with their frowns and sighs, their chuckles and hesitations, their grimaces, gestures and emphases, may all or nearly all be intended as *experimental*, in that they may be things said and done just in case they may elicit fresh and even constructive responses, or flush old stagnancies away.

And now, what is for us of central importance, precisely the same can be true of things that the still baffled Pythagoras unconfidently mutters in solitude to himself, or dubiously scrawls and re-scrawls to himself in the sand. These too can be heuristic experiments, moves made in the dark, in the faint but not foolish hope that they may prove to be self-proddings forward. Our question, 'With what heuristic intention?' can have for its correct answer, 'In order to try out whether or not it has eye-opening, memory-flogging, or cramp-easing potencies.'

In the children's classroom much of the teacher's saying has to be untentative and unexploratory because it is didactically-intended saying. The teacher himself is in no darkness or twilight at all. But when he is interestedly discussing with colleagues or pupils issues the solutions of which, and even the procedures of solving which, are still out of his own and their reach, then he is exploring and not shepherding. Even his tones of voice are now unsure, but questing. Philosophers all too often forget that not all saying is informing, instructing, correcting, persuading, or reminding. In discussions, things said are said 'on appro', as things quite likely, but not certain, to come to nothing; not told but experimentally mooted. They are like speculations, not investments.

In bad Whodunits the fictional sleuth's mind is described as moving like a well oiled machine. Epistemologists are sometimes similarly guilty of describing Thought, or anyhow the Thought of Logical Thinkers, as moving in a clockwork-like goosestep via already certified premises that are already properly marshalled, to an unavoidable and true conclusion. What the logician's blackboard displays in its symmetrical chalked columns is taken to depict the way in which something

called 'logical thinking' progresses. But this is another utter
fable. Pathfinding is not and cannot be path-following.
Pondering is precisely *not* knowing what steps to take, but
taking tentative steps all the same in order to learn something
from their fate.

Then is Thinking just talking to oneself? Or is it doing
something Extra? Not the former, since our Pythagoras might let
his mind wander and just be reciting under his breath random
and miscellaneous things like anecdotes, Spanish proverbs,
lines from Shakespeare, jingles, and bits of the
multiplication-table; and then he would not be thinking. But
when *Le Penseur* is trying fairly hard to solve his problem, then
what he says to himself, like what you and I say in our
discussions of, perhaps, the same problems, is said, more often
than not quite unsuccessfully, with the governing experimental
purpose of trying by saying it to elicit some forward movement
from himself. And this is not *just* saying things to himself, nor
yet is it doing Something Else as Well. It is saying things to
himself with a special governing purpose, with a specially
directed vigilance, resolution, interest, readiness for failure, and
so on.

Thinking, then, can be saying-things-tentatively-to-oneself
with the specific heuristic intention of trying, by saying them, to
open one's own eyes, to consolidate one's own grasp, or to get
oneself out of a rut; and it is this very specific, experimental
intention that is obliterated by the sweeping generic slogans
'Thought is Language', 'All thinking is in Bits of Language',
'Thinking is Saying Things to Oneself', supplemented or not by
'. . . and Something Else as Well'.

Consider for a moment what it is to do something
experimentally. A boy experimentally turns a tap by turning the
tap, and not by doing this and doing something else as well. Yet,
it may be, though he successfully turns the tap, that his
experiment is a failure since a power cut prevents him from
seeing what happens when he turns the tap. Our adverb
'experimentally' added not an extra action but the specific
intention-to-find-out-what-happens-when-the-tap-is-turned.
Notice that our adverb 'experimentally' cannot reappear in this
'when' clause, a fact for which our Reductionist as well as our
Duplicationist cannot account. They had tried to tell us what
pondering is, eluding that little knot of subordinate clauses, such

as' . . . in order to . . .', 'what happens . . .', and '. . . when . . .', without which the notion of *experimenting* cannot be unpacked; no more than burglary, treaty-signing, or goal-scoring can deliberately be described in simple adjectives *plus* simple verbs, whether mundane or transcendent. What qualifies an undertaking as one of pondering or, not very differently, as one of discussing, is not any catalogue of simple qualities and simple relations, whether rude or refined, but some nexus of statable because statement-shaped conditions.

6

Mowgli in Babel

Reg Cogitans[1] is a stimulating and exasperating book. Again and again Vendler makes new breaks through the crusts of meaning-theory, epistemology and Cartesian exegesis; and then; through these breaks, pulls out plums that had rotted off their trees many summers ago. Out of his valuable improvements upon Austin's locutionary taxonomy he rehashed the most romantic things in the *Memo* and the *Meditations*. In Chomsky's wake, he effectively assails Skinnerian stimulus-response learning-theory; but then, in Chomsky's wake, he surrenders learning-theory to Skinner, finding a shelter for just a few epistemic pets in a Darwinianized doctrine of racial concept-inheritance that is, *pace* Chomsky, unfenced even from Book I of Locke's *Essay*. Vendler's powerful chapter 'On What One Knows' blocks for good current attempts to reduce knowing to an *élite* suburb of believing; yet the book's central concept of *Thinking* is so glued to the 'that . . .'-clause that thinking is, by implication, denied to Beethoven and Capablanca, as well as to us when doing our undoctrinal car-driving, translating, verse-composing and *aporia*-tackling.

Vendler begins by revising and, in one important matter, correcting Austin's botany of speech-act-varieties in general and of performative expressions in particular. I can, in the act of saying something to you, indicate what is the particular species of my saying with such vocal signals as 'I promise you that . . .' and 'May I remind you that . . .?', lest you treat my utterance as a mere forecast or a mere anecdote. But it had been a mistake, due to one misinterpreted similarity of tensing and to another of unchallengeability, to group with such performative signals of specific communicative intent our avowals of cognitive attitude like 'I believe . . .', 'I know . . .', 'I surmise . . .'. 'I doubt whether . . .' and so on. Reminding is doing a normally vocal thing, which

might be whispered and might be performatively signalled by
'May I remind you that . . .?' But recollecting is not doing a vocal
thing; it could not be whispered or performatively 'flagged'.
Verbs of thinking, etc., are not (save for a few jokers) verbs of
saying, or paraphrasable by them. On the other hand, where a
cognitive avowal fits, there a performatively flaggable,
indicative, interrogative or imperative (etc.) sentence also fits. 'I
wonder . . .' is to be completed by an indirect question; 'I foresee
. . .' by an indicative sentence in the future tense. A thought *is*
not a communication, but it is what a communicative vehicle of
it conveys. Here the pumpkin, there the barrow.

So Vendler, now moving independently of Austin, draws up
two sub-classified lists, namely: List A of performatively usable
verbs of saying, like *tell, promise, request, warn, suggest, remind,*
etc., and (necessarily paralleling List A) List B of verbs for
cognitive states, acts, attitudes, etc., like *think that, believe, realize,
know, fancy, recall, anticipate, wonder, doubt,* etc. Already, by page
36, Vendler is declaring that 'the domain of propositional verbs
reveals a staggering perspective: the almost universal identity of
the objects of speech and thought.' ('Identity' is elsewhere
prudently replaced by (parallelism' and 'isomorphism'. The
barrow and the pumpkin fit each other, but the barrow is not
edible, nor is the pumpkin steerable.) Our own staggerings are
moderated when we notice that Vendler's listed verbs of saying
and his listed verbs of thinking have both been selected
precisely for their dedication to the 'that . . .-complement' or the
'wh . . .-complement'. We hear almost nothing of such verbs of
saying as: *recite, echo, quote, chant, rehearse, interject, prompt,
chatter, chat, converse, soliloquize, curse, jeer, carol, scold, abuse,
grumble, mutter, shout, render, mispronounce, lecture, deliver,* etc.;
and we hear almost nothing of such thought-verbs as: *ponder,
ruminate, meditate, revolve, deliberate, dwell on, reconsider, weigh,
canvass, debate, tackle, study, examine, analyse, survey, sift, calculate,
compose, design, check, work out, try out, flounder,* etc. *Le Penseur's*
pondering does not qualify as Vendler's 'thought'.

More than this. Not only does Vendler find with amazement
his chosen pumpkins isomorphic with his chosen barrows, but
he suddenly derives from these matchings an exciting
ontological and epistemological dualism (p. 39). 'The total
import of the emerging picture is clear enough. Man lives in two
environments, in two worlds: as a "body", "an extended thing",

he is among objects and events in the physical, spatio-temporal universe; as a "mind", a "thinking thing", he lives and communes with objects of a different kind, which he also perceives, acquires, holds and offers in various ways to other citizens of this world, to other minds.' Just because the barrow *is* not its pumpkin, the barrow is relegated to the backyard, while the pumpkin luxuriates in Eden.

Against well-patronized reductions of Thought to Language, of Thinking to Saying, of Propositions to Sentences, of Concepts to Words, of Meanings to Symbols, Vendler manoeuvres forcibly and effectively. The adverb-tolerances, *inter alia*, of verbs of thinking are systematically disparate from those verbs of saying. I cannot, in logical grammar, know, believe, surmise or disprove something sluggishly or hurriedly; either in a Yorkshire or in a non-Yorkshire accent. You and I may think alike without your having a smattering of my English. Premises and conclusions are neither Yiddish nor Esperanto, neither ungrammatical nor grammatical, neither hesitant nor glib. And so on. The reductions of these ø's to being 'Nothing-But-ø's' collapse. But then Vendler, like Chomsky, follows up his demolition of the 'Nothing But' by having the timeworn recourse to the 'Something Else As Well'. Unaffected by the forcible and effective manoeuvres of a Quine, say, against the duplicationisms of a Plato, a Descartes or a Bolzano, Vendler requisitions the hackneyed Two Worlds, the Two Mes, the Two Acts and (for the 'sources' of our concepts), the Two 'Froms . . .'. Of course, his 'Two . . .' is no worse, but it is also no better than, say, Quine's 'Only One . . .'. Cross-category counting yields neither a couple nor a singleton of 'them', where there can be no 'they'. A soldier obeys the order to halt. The behaviourist witnesses just the One bodily act of halting, with no obeying; the Cartesian adds one piece of obeying to one act of halting and gets Two . . .– well! Two *whats?* How many do the top of the tree and the tree make? A Platonic Two? Two *whats?* How many do the ball-kicking and the goal-scoring make? A Quinean only One? Only One *what?*

Chapter IV, 'On What One Knows', strikes an unimpartial reader as the most powerful chapter in the book. It is new and right. Except to some extent in method, it stands apart from the rest of the book. Associationism, empiricism and behaviourism do not, for once, raise their Skinner-like heads; nor does angelic rationalism brandish against them its flaming French sword. Cartesian dualism and innatism are given a half-holiday. Chomsky is left behind.

With great success Vendler attacks, root and branch, any theory that defines *knowledge* in terms of *belief*. So far is knowledge from being belief qualified as (1) true, (2) held with full conviction, (3) well-founded, (*plus* any other leak-stoppers), that knowledge and belief do not even have the same 'objects'. I may indeed know that tomorrow is May 1, and you may believe that tomorrow is May 1. But while I know (or do not know) what the date is tomorrow, or tomorrow's date, you cannot, in grammar, believe or doubt what the date is tomorrow, or tomorrow's date. The calendar-fact that tomorrow is May 1 can be something that I have (or have not) been taught or told, that I have (or have not) learned or discovered; but this calendar-fact cannot, in grammar, be something that I do (or do not) believe, or something that someone has (or has not) half-convinced me of. Ceasing to know something is forgetting it; but ceasing to believe something is not forgetting it. Being ignorant of something is not being unconvinced of it. Nor, as Plato knew, is teaching a variety of persuading. Rhetoricians are not, as such, instructors. Except in its peripheral sense of 'authentic', 'true', while a proper epithet of, *inter alia*, beliefs, opinions, conjectures, theories, etc., is not one of knowledge. I can know the *Odyssey*, even by heart, while doubting whether an Odysseus ever listened to any Sirens singing. But I cannot believe the *Odyssey* while doubtful of its truth, much less 'believe it by heart'. For I cannot, in grammar, believe-how-the-story-goes, as I can know-how-the-story-goes. 'Know' can, but 'believe' cannot carry an indirect question; and 'know' can, but 'believe' cannot (with an obvious reservation) govern a substantive, like a place-name, a play-title, a route, a person's nickname, etc. It is not from scepticism that you cannot believe the Greek alphabet. This is not a grammatically possible object of belief, doubt and persuasion, as it is of knowledge and ignorance, of teaching and learning, of studying and forgetting.

Vendler might have borrowed ammunition from this source. To disbelieve is to refuse to *accept* something *from* a person (or from an impersonal authority or source). It is verb of reception-from . . . . Being disbelieved is the fate not of propositions, but of *sources* of propositions – President Nixon, perhaps, or *The Times*. 'Credence', 'credulity', 'incredulous', 'discredit', 'believer', 'faith', 'sceptical', 'trust', 'mistrust', etc., still connote this inter-personal element of acceptance or non-acceptance *from* . . . . With 'believe' the position is complex. 'I do (or do not) believe you (or *The Times*)' remains as comfortable as 'I disbelieve you (or *The Times*)'. But 'believe that . . .' has for a long time *also* been as comfortable as 'think that . . .' and 'suppose that . . .', where 'disbelieve that . . .' still hurts our ears. Anyhow, whether or not because of the verb's original sense of 'accept *from* . . .', the 'object' of belief is in many important ways a defendent on trial. It may have the very highest credentials, but unlike knowledge, it does require credentials. A belief gives off the smell and the rustling sound of commercial 'paper' that still has to be cashed on the real world. It *is* not that cash, which may yet turn out not to be there. But what someone knows is not 'paper' but his real estate, his hard cash, his consumable goods, not just his paper-credit, however good. You can always query whether he *does* know it, but you cannot concede that he is the possessor, and still wonder whether the property exists out there in the world. The objectivity that belongs to the very 'objects of knowledge' themselves is only desiderated, however confidently, for the 'objects of belief'.

Hence we ask 'Why do you believe . . .?', requesting credentials, and not 'Why do you know . . .?'; and we ask 'How do you know . . .?', requesting the acquisition-procedure, and not 'How do you believe . . .?'.

In Chapter VI, 'Word and Concept', Vendler develops and in some respects diverges from Chomsky's doctrine of 'innate ideas', that is of the un-learnedness of certain basic parts of our knowledge. 'Not in entire forgetfulness, And not it utter nakedness, But trailing clouds of [Universal grammar] do we come . . .'.

One rather phoney puzzle to be solved by the Chomsky–Vendler theory of concept-inheritance is how the quite ordinary child, still in the nursery, masters so swiftly the essentials of his mother-tongue, both its basic vocabulary and especially its basic syntax. Equip him from birth (but only 'implicitly') with the structure that underlies all the different particular tongues and dialects alike, and then it is supposed at once to become quite unpuzzling that, still in the nursery, the child so rapidly implements this abstract syntactical and semantic schema with the non-innate particular vocabulary and, especially, the non-innate particular constructions that are peculiar to his mother-tongue. Says Vendler dogmatically (p. 126) 'It is impossible to learn a language word by word from scratch, that is without the possession of a previous language or of a structure [sic] more or less isomorphic with one.' The child '. . . . must learn his native tongue in a way similar to the way one learns a second language. He must have . . . a native equipment that codes the fundamental . . . features of any possible human language' (p. 140). 'Such a system of native "ideas" provides the framework which is then filled up progressively through the influence of a more specific code representing the features of the mother tongue' (p. 140). '. . . the same concept and the same thought can be echoed in the various languages *and* [N.B.] in the "code", as yet unknown, operating in the human nervous system' (p. 142). Chomsky, in his *Language and Mind* and *Cartesian Linguistics*, had not made these with-it, but still shocking, drafts on communication-theory. Codes presuppose language, as shop-stewards presuppose employees. The child or the grown-up in talking and following talk is *not* encoding or decoding. Nor, *a fortiori*, is he misencoding or misdecoding (liabilities that are passed over). Conversely, Vendler wisely omits Chomsky's absurd assimilation of the toddling language-learner's task to that theory-constructing according to formalized inductive procedures of 'heuristic methods' by which working scientists are reverently hamstrung.

What parts of our knowledge are innate or unacquired? Vendler's candidates differ interestingly from Chomsky's. Chomsky stocks us up from our starts almost solely with universal grammar, i.e. some innate apparatus of schemata impartially underlying the surface constructions of our differing daily English or French sentences; some deep 'mental' structures according to which we organize the superficially differing verbal expressions of our thoughts. But Vendler, thinking a good deal more of vocabulary-items than of syntax structures, nominates the 'clear and distinct ideas', which 'are "*a priori*"' in origin and self-contained in their development' of *asserting, requesting, believing, deciding, truth, necessity, person, object, process, state, change, purpose, causation, time, number* (p. 141). This quaint *mêlée* of inborn concepts is later (pp. 176–7) reinforced with Descartes' and Chomsky's blessed *triangle* (miscredited also to the *Meno*). 'No experience is relevant to one's idea of' any of these things, whereas our 'empirical' ideas, like that of 'dog' remain 'open to experience'. These deviant uses of 'relevant' and 'open' are left cryptic, or worse.

What seems to have gone wrong is this. Chomsky and Vendler, with many others, began by assuming that Pavlov, Skinner, and that ilk have worked out, or, at least, are working out, the scientific and therefore mechanical theory of learning. Pavlov's imprisoned and strait-jacketed dog, in salivating each time the bell rings, exhibits the results of training under laboratory conditions. Same stimulus, same responses. But then Chomsky attends seriously to the crucial fact that the human language-learner rapidly becomes able to originate un-precedented sentences and to follow the, for him, novel sentences originated by others. Same stimuli (or no stimuli) and indefinitely variegated responses! We do not talk mech-anically. So (notice the argument) *since* to learn is to be Pavlovianly conditioned, therefore the language-learner does not *learn* to talk and to follow talk. Instead of sitting back to think ecologically (and not hydraulically) about learning, teaching, training, showing, stimulating, correcting, guiding, leading, emulating, etc., Chomsky, Vendler and Co. surrender the whole notion of learning to the mechanizers, and make do, as best they can, with the notion of evolutionary inheritance. As live talking is not a hydraulic output, *therefore* it is a bit of a trailing cloud of biological glory. It is no accident that in Vendler's *Res Cogitans* the words 'teach', 'instruct' and 'train' hardly occur. The verbs 'help', 'encourage' and 'guide' seem never to occur. Like Pavlov's tortured dog, the toddler is supposed to be just 'exposed' to alien noises, a Mowgli, unfostered and alone (but under irreproachable laboratory conditions) in Babel. The things that actually once went on at Vendler's own mother's knee and in Vendler's own nursery are totally ignored; and even the English child's learning of his second language, French, say, is described as the effect of his hearing talk *in English* about the French language (p. 145). In that real life that Chomsky and Vendler are too scientific, or too un-ecological, to recognize, Tommy ordinarily has a mother, father, brothers, sisters, uncles, aunts and playmates. Some of them are (hush!) actually fond of him, as he is of them. They like helping him and bringing him on; he demands and delights in their intended and unintended guidances, examples and stimulations. They sing to him, and then with him; they recite to him and then prompt his return-recitations to them; they provide, wittingly and unwittingly, what he models his own actions, accents, intonations and nascent phrases on; they challenge him, race him, practise him, test him and correct him; at first in slow time, and then in quick time, they *show* him the delivery of rhymes, numerals, letters of the alphabet, street-names; they applaud and laugh at his earliest puns and word-coinages; they feed his nascent hunger for consecutive prose with bed-time stories; and they listen with fond patience to his own first self-invented stories. Their disappointing misunderstandings and non-understandings of him teach him to try to employ safeguards against such disappointments; following their examples he tries to avoid or correct equivocations, ellipses and indefinitenesses. In their ritualized games, impersonations and ceremonies he learns to insist that the *right* syllables and the *right* steps and gestures are produced by others and by himself. He listens or half-listens to what the grown-ups say to each other, and then, not always felicitously, parrots their words in their tones of voice. As Aristotle said, what we have to do when we have learned to do it, we learn to do by doing it; thus it is, in large measure, that Tommy learns to converse, narrate, describe, catalogue, count, complain, argue, and so on. Here is the actual language-learning and the actual language-teaching that precede his formal schooling and continue alongside it. Same input, same output? Rubbish! But what of '[Tommy] cannot know at birth which language he is to learn, but he must know that its grammar must be of a predetermined form that excludes many imaginable languages. Having selected a permissible hypothesis, he [Tommy!] can use inductive evidence for corrective action, confirming or disconfirming his choice.' etc., etc. (*Language and Mind*, p. 78). Here too – Rubbish! Does he learn hide-and-seek, snap and football by solitary inductions? Or does he learn to play initially strange but thrilling games with other children by wholeheartedly playing them?

Can Tommy learn from this sociable family-teaching that universal grammar and basic vocabulary which he assuredly, as Chomsky saw and proved, would not have acquired from the rational stimuli of Skinner's unsociable laboratory? Let us not even debate this issue until we are told whether or not the phrase 'universal grammar' is being used, like the philosophers' 'logical grammar', metaphorically. Is this 'underlying *deep structure*, . . . a system of categories and phrases' (*Language and Mind*, p. 25) really a system of categories or really one of phrases? It cannot be both. Are the 'innate mental structures' structures of inscribables or of introspectables? They cannot be both.

The last and longest chapter of *Res Cogitans* is a survey of Descartes' epistemology. Vendler's deep sympathy with Cartesian dualism and innatism, together with his relish for Descartes' occasional Chomsky-like sentiments about unmechanical human speech, make for a penetrating, if sometimes incautious, exegesis and for a few slanted renderings of Descartes' French and Latin. But the chapter is really fertile in new ideas about usually underestimated elements of Descartes' thought, as well as in illuminating parallels with, and divergences from, Vendler's own thoughts. In particular Vendler's idiosyncratic notion of Thought as a cinematographic sequence of instantaneous mental exposures to propositions makes some of Descartes' statements about Thought seem by comparision pretty reasonable.

Res Cogitans is at once a stimulating and exasperating book; it should not be missed but neither should it be swallowed.

NOTE

1 *Res Cogitans: An Essay in Rational Psychology*, by Zeno Vendler (Cornell University Press, 1972).

7

Negative 'Actions'

(1) Whatever I am now doing, there are infinitely many other things that I am not now doing. I am not sneezing, mountain-climbing, telephoning in Russian, cooking, composing a sonnet, . . . This is no more interesting than the fact that whatever the date may be today, there are infinitely many other dates that it is not; or the fact that wherever the snowflake did fall, there are infinitely many other places where it did not fall.

(2) There are many kinds of actions that we perform in order that things may be *not* the case which otherwise would or might be the case. They can be called 'nullifying acts'. Of this kind are acts of *obstructing, resisting, hindering, refusing, demurring, dissuading, repudiating, rescinding, cancelling, forbidding, hiding, disguising, erasing, purging, scrubbing, correcting, recanting, unfastening, unravelling, sacking, dismantling, sheltering, weeding, liberating* . . . The actions are positive and witnessable actions, but what is achieved by them, when successful, is that specifiable might-have-been states of affairs do *not* obtain. (Note that what is, say, rescinded may itself be the prohibition of something; and the prohibited something could have been the unfastening or erasing of something.) This point is also rather uninteresting, and the more so since it is often an arbitrary matter whether the result of an action is to count as positive or negative. Is it the door's being open or its being shut that is the negative state of affairs? The sponge's being wet or its being dry?

(3) What is interesting is the class of acts (if they *are* acts) which consist in the agent's intentional *non*-performance of some specifiable actions. For example, I *postpone* writing a letter if, without having forgotten the task, I do not write the letter now, although I could write it now. I cannot, in this sense,

postpone *your* letter-writing. The teetotaller and the vegetarian regularly and deliberately *abstain* from partaking of available alcohol and meat. This class of negative 'acts' (if they *are* acts) includes *refraining, abstaining, postponing, shirking, neglecting, disobeying, overlooking, condoning, forgiving, acquiescing, ignoring, idling, pausing, resting, hesitating, omitting, enduring, waiting, remaining, permitting, letting, keeping, (still* or *a secret), holding (one's tongue), sparing, economizing, relinquishing, yielding, relying, trusting, . . .* A few of these things can be 'done' unintentionally and by inanimate agents; the snow can *remain* on the hilltop, though not patiently or impatiently; the wind can *pause* for a moment, but not for a rest. Or are these metaphors?

When we first consider these and other candidates for the status of 'negative actions', we feel rebellious. Surely *procrastinating,* so far from being the doing of something, is rather the not-doing-it-yet of something. I should not be *resting* if I were thereby exerting myself.

Let us first assemble reasons in favour of classing negative 'actions' with actions proper, and then assemble the reasons against so classifying them.

REASONS IN FAVOUR

We directly contrapose sins of commission to sins of *omission.* We observe most of the Ten Commandments by religiously *avoiding* doing specified things. I can be commanded, requested and advised as well to *pause* as to move on; I may be punished for my *negligences* as well as for my active misdeeds. I can intend and even endeavour to *tolerate* or *forgive* something, and the task may be too much for me. I may, with alacrity or reluctance, *permit* something. Like any other promise, my promise to *wait* or to *keep your secret* may be broken or kept.

Some of the temporal qualifications that commonly attach to ordinary positive actions, attach also to negative 'actions' though there are some interesting discrepancies too. I began to *rest* at 3 p.m. and went on until 4 p.m.; I was *holding my tongue* off and on throughout the difficult interview. On the other hand it was not suddenly or gradually, quickly or slowly, that I *postponed* writing the letter or *waited* for the train; and while I might have blabbed at this or at that moment, it could not have been at a moment but only through moments, or even through weeks, that I was *keeping* the secret. Like the positive action of singing a song, a negative 'action' seems often to be a duration-occupant; yet unlike singing a song, a negative 'action', like *waiting* or *acquiescing*, does not seem to fill its duration up with anything. Even the behaviourist eye-witness could not see or hear anything in particular continuously going on or being done during the duration of the wait or the acquiescence.

REASONS AGAINST

(1) Ordinary positive actions commonly admit of characterization as skilful or clumsy, efficient or inefficient, etc. I might by taking tuition or by practising make myself better at doing them. But negative 'actions' seem not to earn good or bad marks for their techniques. It is a bad thing to *default* or *condone*; it is a good thing to *forgive* or *keep a secret*; but, apart from his ingenuity in camouflaging his 'act', the 'agent' seems here to have no openings for proficiencies.

(2) Ordinary actions often require, or are helped by, special materials and implements. I write my letter on paper with pen and ink, or with pencil; or in type, or in Braille, etc. But for *postponing* writing my letter I need no materials or implements; postponing writing is, in part, intentionally *not*-using-writing-materials-yet. The stay-at-home needs neither the traveller's means of transport nor any counterpart means of *staying at home*.

(3) We do many things by means of doing auxiliary things. The mother lulls her baby to sleep partly by singing; the window-cleaner polishes the glass partly by rubbing. But there is nothing in particular by doing which I await the train. I may indeed amuse myself during my wait by trying, maybe in vain, to solve the crossword-puzzle; but I do not thereby try in vain to wait.

(4) In his article 'Dramatic representations' (*Philosophical Quarterly*, Oct. 1972) J. O. Urmson shows how one and the same

action can be, at bottom-level, one for example, of making ink-marks on paper; at second-level, one of writing a letter; at third-level, one of offering one's resignation. The higher-level action cannot be executed unless some action or other of the next lower level is executed, and this is therefore relatively basic to that higher-level action. Preaching thus requires, but does not reduce to, the voicing of vowels and consonants. Negative 'actions', on the contrary, such as *acquiescing, permitting* and *abstaining* seem not to rest on any such derivatively purposed *infra*-actions. Where the preacher had (*infra*) to voice vowels and consonants if he was (*supra*) to deliver his sermon, there is no corresponding *infra*-x-ing without which the climber could not have *paused,* the policeman could not have *let* the traffic move on, or the non-smoker could not have done his *non-smoking.* Certainly the non-smoker cannot be *merely* non-smoking; things will be being done, said, proceeding or happening in his 'inner' and in his outer life while he is non-smoking. But there is nothing in particular, internal or external, which he must have been doing, such that he *supra*-kept-off-tobacco by *infra*-doing this.

This at first surprising point is nothing more than an application of a familiar point about negation in general. Though the householder who is not at home cannot be nowhere, the notice 'Not at home' does not specify anything more about his particular whereabouts than would the notice 'somewhere else than at home'. Save for 'Not heads = tails, and *vice versa*', not-x . . .' *ex officio* abjures particularities. The negativing title or description of a negative 'action' specifies only that one particular thing that the agent is *not* doing, smoking, for instance, or moving away from the train's arrival platform, or continuing climbing; it is non-committal about what else in particular he is doing. Similarly, the order 'Do not wear uniform' tacitly permits any alternative costume you please. Lots of people may obey this order whose costumes differ from one another in all possible ways, except the one negative way.

So our negative 'actions' seem not to qualify as actions proper, for the reason that the full story of a positive action would report it with its full complement of *inter alia* chronological, behavioural, technical, circumstantial details, while the full story of a negative 'action' would be specific only about the particular thing that the agent did *not* do. Moreover, although we have no regulations laying down the maximum duration of a single action, still some negative 'actions', like keeping a secret for a lifetime, or submitting to oppression for twenty years, are surely too protracted to be granted action-status. What of my postponement for three hours of my letter-writing? Or for ten minutes? Partly similarly, while no regulation stipulates how many different unautomatic actions a person might be doing at the same time – two? four or five? – there is no limit to the number of negative 'actions' that he may be 'doing' during the same period. There he is, keeping ten different secrets, resting from his climbing, postponing replying to a question, overlooking a discourtesy and abstaining from food, drink and tobacco!

We may imagine the Behaviourist trying to discern exactly what visibly or audibly distinguishes the man on the platform who is waiting for his train from the man on the platform who is taking shelter from the sleet. For both may be reading their newspapers and smoking their pipes; they may be fidgeting and looking about them in similar ways. The big differences between their purposes seem alas! to be behaviourally occult differences.

This occultness at first gratifies the Cartesian. He is, however, soon disconcerted when told that the two men on the platform had resembled one another not only in their muscular conduct, but also in their 'inward' meditations, reminiscings, expectations, boredoms, reactions to the news and daydreams about their gardens and their holidays. The big differences between their purposes seem, alas! not to consist in even introspectible or retrospectible differences.

Both our Behaviourist and our Cartesian can now take comfort from this interim result of ours, namely that negative 'actions' are not actions. When we have heard that someone is now neglecting his garden, or now resting from his climb, we have not heard what in particular he is now doing, any more than his 'not at home' told us where in particular the householder then was. So waiting is neither an overt nor an 'inner' action; idling is neither a witnessable nor an unwitnessable action.

Then what *are* our negative 'actions' if they are not actions?

DISPOSITIONS?

First we should dismiss one philosophically tempting category-suggestion. Our negative 'actions' are not dispositions or *hexeis*. The teetotaller's lifelong abstinence may indeed be a character-trait, a self-discipline, a habit or even a phobia. But it is excercised in his actual tense-determinate abstainings, for example in his conscientiously refusing this particular drink-offer. Keeping a secret in a particular contingency or through a particular stretch of time may be difficult or easy; but it is not difficult or easy to be *able* to keep secrets or to be *prone* to betray them. Negative 'actions', though not actions, are nonetheless actualities, and not potentialities, capacities, skills, tastes, pronenesses or weaknesses. The traveller's patient or impatient waiting *is* not his patient or impatient nature. At most it is a particular short-term exhibition of it; and it need not even be that. But actualities of what sort or sorts?

CONSCIOUSNESS

Before directly tackling the question, What then is a negative 'action' if it is neither an action nor a disposition? we need to notice, without much discussion, something that it shares with anything else which is both an actuality and an 'intentional' one. A person who is postponing something, permitting something or holding something back, must be doing this consciously or wittingly. Indeed his doing it must incorporate, in some way (*what* way?) the 'thought' of the very retort which he is holding back, or of the very bit of letter-writing which he is deferring until later. He cannot need to be informed or even to be reminded either that he has a secret to keep or what the secret is – or else he is not still refraining from divulging that particular secret. On the other hand our secret-keeper or even our temporarily procrastinating letter-writer cannot be supposed to be thinking about nothing else than his *not*-blabbing or his *not*-writing throughout the minutes or the months of its duration. He cannot be meditating always and he need not be meditating often or for long at a time, or even at all, about his commitment or his dereliction. The statesman taking his needed fishing-holiday would lose both the pleasure and the benefits of his loch-side vacation if he did not succeed in putting aside all thoughts of what had been occupying him and will be occupying him in his Department. But of course he is well aware, in some other way – but *what* way? – of what his fishing is being a blessed respite from – well aware of it, yet without its being on his mind. It need not pluck at even the fringes of his attention.

This, however, is not a suitable juncture for an inquest on the notions of *awareness* and/or *consciousness*. Whatever the result of such an inquest, it will apply to our negative 'actions' no less than to our ordinary positive doings, sayings, ponderings, calculatings, regrettings, etc.

OF A HIGHER ORDER

Whatever our negative 'actions' may turn out categorially to be, it is useful to realize from the start that they are of a higher order than the actions of which they are the avoidances or deferments in very much the same way as that in which, inside the theory of meaning, some propoundables are notoriously of a higher order than some other propoundables.

For example, the truth or falsehood *today is not Friday* is of a higher order than *today is Friday*, since the former is one particular 'operation upon' the latter, namely a repudiation of it. It could have been worded 'Today Friday? No!' To insist that *today is after all Friday* would be to repudiate such a repudiation, and its wording could non-reduntantly contain two 'nots'. The argument *Today is Friday, so tomorrow is Saturday* – likewise the conditional statement *it will be Saturday tomorrow, if it is Friday today*, and the disjunction *either it was Friday yesterday or it is Friday today* are other 'operations upon' the minimally sophisticated or lowest order truth or falsehood *today is Friday*. A child who could not yet understand this *infra*-proposition *a fortiori* could not understand the other *supra*-propositions. Notice that for a person to deny that today is Friday it is not necessary that he or anyone else should actually have averred that today is Friday. He could be repudiating either an actual assertion or a merely possible suggestion to this effect.

This ladder of orders – which is not limited to only two rungs

– was needed for, *inter alia,* the dissolution of the paradoxes of self-reference. The sentence 'What this very sentence says is false' purports to convey a true allegation of falsity against itself, and so to tell the truth on condition that it tells a falsehood, and *vice versa.* The book would *be* its own book-review, and so be at once of a higher and of a lower order than itself.

We now need to see how these higher/lower-order differences extend far beyond the circuit of propoundables and cover also our non-communicative purposes, intentions and endeavours.

(A) How does my act of lifting the log out of the way of my bicycle differ from the soldier's muscularly similar act of lifting the log in obedience to the sergeant's command to do so? It differs not just in purpose, but in purpose-order. For the soldier means – '*supra*-means' – to do whatever the sergeant commands; only derivatively does he mean – '*infra*-mean' – to lift the log *qua* being what, as it happens, the sergeant commands. A statement of the soldier's intention would contain only in a subordinate clause a mention of log-lifting. The *supra*-act of obedient log-lifting is of a higher order, and so is on a higher rung of sophistication than its *infra*-act of log-lifting. Incidentally, for Epimenidean reasons, the sergeant would have been unwise not only to bellow 'Obey this very command' or Disobey this very command'; but even to bellow 'Lift that log obediently'.

(B) A boy makes an *experimental* jump with the higher order purpose of finding out how far he can jump (*not* how far he can jump experimentally). He may be *infra*-trying to clear the stream, but he is also *supra*-trying to settle thereby a researcher's problem about his own jumping capacities. His friend who gives him a helping shove lengthens the jump but ruins the experiment. The success/failure conditions of the *infra*- and the *supra*-endeavours are different, though there is only one jump to be counted. Stream-clearing enters, but only subordinately, into the programme of his experiment.

(C) The singer is today rehearsing his German song in order to improve not, of course, this rehearsal but his concert-singing tomorrow. Today's rehearsal is a failure if tomorrow's concert-singing is bad; it is wasted if the concert is cancelled. A mention of tomorrow's concert-performance would have to have a place in a report of what the singer is today *supra*-trying to accomplish by means, *inter alia*, of *infra*-trying today to articulate clearly his German words; and a cancellation of the concert would not falsify this report. Practising anything incorporates – but how? – the 'thought' of what is being practised for; but what the thought is the thought of can be problematical and even, in the event, counterfactual.

It is obvious that our negative 'actions' do, in the required way, constitute one particular species of higher order 'operations upon' lower order positive actions. The positive *infra*-actions of eating flesh and divulging the secret are intentionally left unexecuted by the vegetarian and the confidant; the statement of their *supra*-purposes in devouring fruit and in tongue-holding would subordinately mention flesh-eating and secret-blabbing. Nothing extra need be done or said from which our behaviourist witness could discriminate the fruit-eating of the vegatarian from that of his non-vegetarian neighbour; or the tongue-holdings of the repository of the secret from the silences of his companion who merely has nothing to say.

There is a not quite obvious precaution that we need to take here, a pracaution with which Russell has familiarized us in particular connection with the significations of expressions that are or could be nominative to verbs of existence or non-existence. What I bite or sell must be there for me to bite or sell it; what I see or recollect must be, or have been, there for me to see or recollect it. In such cases the accusative to the transitive verb designates an actual action-correlate which possesses an endless catalogue of (often unknown) properties, relations, dimensions, concomitants, etc., of its own. It abides our questions. But what I predict, hope for or believe to have been the case may *not* be 'there'. The predicted sea-battle may not be fought and the hoped-for meeting may not take place, and then there are no answers at all to detail-questions about, for instance the casualties incurred in that predicted battle or about the refreshments enjoyed at that hoped-for meeting. 'The battle was not fought.' 'But what is an unfought battle?' 'The meeting was cancelled.' 'Were only nobodies present at it, then?'

When, using a technical phrase, we said that a higher order assertion, purpose, etc., was an 'operation upon' a lower order assertion, purpose, etc., we risked being misled by the fact that a surgical operation does have for its 'object' an actual or real-live correlate, namely a patient with a career, name, income and history of his own. But while our boy's experimental jumping did have to contain at least one actual jump, our singer's rehearsal of his German song did not require that the concert rehearsed for actually took place. The ordered log-lifting was left unexecuted by the disobedient soldier.

To apply all this now directly to our negative 'actions', it stands out that abstaining from alcohol requires the *non*-partaking of alcohol; postponing the letter-writing requires *not* writing it yet; and permitting the children to paddle requires *not* prohibiting, preventing or hindering their paddling. Mentions of abstainings, postponings and permittings specify things that could-have-been-done but were not actually done, so, in a way, they do mention inexecuted actions. Of course, 'unexecuted action' sounds like a contradiction, as did our 'unfought battle'. But, to employ for once only, an imperfectly fitting technical idiom, our phrases 'predicted battle', 'postponed letter-writing', commanded log-lifting', etc., contains only act-*descriptions*, but not also act-*names*, or act-*designations*. So we can tell precisely what the disobedient soldier did *not* do, without thereby having an actual bit of log-lifting to refer to, or to ask further factual questions about. As log-lifting was shirked, no 'it' occurred, so we have– and God has – no 'it' to refer to. Only the sergeant and the soldier are still 'there' and only the stentorian command was formerly 'there' to be referred to and to have detail-questions asked about them. A person who, hearing that the friend had for years never blabbed the secret, now asks 'How many blabbings did the friend *not* commit?' would be asking as ludicrous a question as 'How many inhabitants does the desert island *not* contain?' There is no counting what is not there, as Plato saw (*Sophist*, 238–9).

All this helps us to trace to its source the, at first puzzling, unconcreteness, that is the factual, circumstantial and behavioural hollowness of our negative 'actions'. It is just a special case of the factual hollowness of *denials* of existance, occurrence or performance, etc. in general. The reason why 'Not at home' fails to fix the house-holder's actual location is the reason why 'waiting' fails to specify what in particular the traveller is actually doing.

LINES OF ACTION

We all know how some, but not all, of our actions belong to lines or courses of actions, and we know what a variety there is of such lines of action. For one unimportant example, a man dieting conducts (not his telephonings, readings, train-catchings but) his eatings according to a complex prescription as to what he should and should not eat, when and in what quantities he should eat it, and for how many days or weeks he should go on so regulating his feeding. Notice that there is nothing that he eats that could not be eaten also by his wife, who is not dieting. There are not foods and *also* dietetic entities, but only the foods-which-are-prescribed-to-him, as opposed to the foods which are forbidden, etc. He and his wife both *infra*-eat their victuals from hunger, politeness, habit, etc.; but unlike her, he eats what he eats (and nothing else) also with the *supra*-purpose of recovering his health by, *inter alia,* observing the stipulated dietary regimen. His lightly boiled egg, unlike hers, is a sanctioned lightly boiled egg; unlike her he eats it hungrily perhaps but also dutifully. All the courses of all his daily meals are, through weeks, conducted by him under the continuing and coordinating *supra*-aegis of what the doctor prescribes. His conduct of his eatings is of a higher order than his or her eatings.

The wording of his dietary prescription has to contain quantifying, negativing and modalizing expressions like 'usually', 'unless', 'never', 'all', 'any', 'some', 'not', 'whenever', 'except when', 'may', 'must', etc., none of which would enter into an observer's report of the egg-eating in which he and his wife are both engaged on a particular occasion. He diets by for instance *never-x-ing,* but he is not now eating his egg by *never-x-ing,* by *sometimes-y-ing* or by *z-ing unless* . . . Dieting is not, as eating an egg is, an action. But nor is it a mere potentiality, liability, etc. It is a sustained actuality, and an intentional one, which goes on perhaps for three weeks. It is realized in the meals actually taken, without itself being an extra meal or an extra dish in any meal; but yet it is not broken off by the intervals between meals, between courses or between swallows, any more than the sermon stops when the preacher pauses between his sentences or his words. Just when is Big Ben actually striking Twelve? We saw that negative 'actions' could similarly be actual, intentional and less or more sustained although non-persistent.

Here is the beginning of an uncompletable catalogue of other kinds of lines or courses of action by which we can abide or from which we can deviate: *policies, routines, traditions, fashions, compacts, trade-practices, codes of manners, conventions, rules of competitions, styles, programmes, ceremonials, professional, social and moral duties,* . . . To follow or adhere to such a line is to do, in intentional accordance with the line, things any one of which could be done without regard to there being such a line. I *could,* on a certain Saturday, mow my lawn without Saturday's being my lawn-mowing day. The girl *could* be wearing a mini-skirt, even if mini-skirts were not yet or still in fashion. We saw that the invalid's wife *could* eat just the foods prescribed for him, without their being prescribed for her. Higher-order purposes generate, not new kinds of actions, but *supra*-conducts of otherwise ordinary *infra*-actions, *infra*-actions which can be performed either with no higher-order intention at all, or else with different ones.

We might now say, in general terms, that a line or course of action is (*a*) a (short or long, closely or loosely packed) sequence of *infra*-actions so conducted as to realize a higher-order purpose; or (*b*) that it is the tenor of such a sequence, that is it is what a deviation from the line is a deviation from. (Compare the course that the ship is actually taking with the course that she is three miles off when she is three miles off course.)

Following a line of conduct, e.g. observing a code of manners or a fashion, is not usually a matter of conducting one's relevant *infra*-actions down a severely constricting tramrail. Five girls may all be in the same fashion whose dresses, hats, ornaments, and coiffures are all attractively different. Even rules of the road give car-drivers some latitudes. Expressions like 'either-or', 'approximately', 'many', 'reasonably soon after', 'near', 'unless', 'if possible', 'may', and 'need not' occur naturally in the wording of a policy, a statute or a piece of technical advice.

It should not be piously supposed that all *supra*-conducts of *infra*-actions are *ipso facto* commendable. Some fashions are deplorable and some policies are disastrous. One doctor scorns the regimen imposed by another; and the citizens of one country quite often despise the loyalties, the manners and the religion of another country.

NEGATIVE 'ACTIONS' AND LINES OF ACTION

It now leaps to the eye that at least plenty of our negative 'actions' qualify well to be assimilated to lines of action of already familiar sorts – with just the specific difference that these will be essentially *negative* lines of action. For a line of action, unlike an action, can, as we have seen, tolerate in its wording such expressions as 'not', 'never', 'either-or', 'if', etc., etc. Vegetarians, like cold-bath-addicts, may be credited with either a policy, or an inveterate routine, or a regimen. But while the cold-bath-addice enacts and perhaps preaches the *positive* maxim 'always take cold baths', the vegetarian enacts and perhaps preaches the *negative* maxim 'do *not* ever eat flesh'. Keeping a friend's secret is hardly general enough to rank as a policy; it need not even be fidelity to a promise. But it is certainly the sustained preservation not only of a definite talk-control but of a negative one. Everything that the confidant allows himself to come out with vocally (or by letter etc.) with whatever *infra*-intentions, he manages also with the mostly latent *supra*-purpose of *not* thereby giving away the secret.

Like plenty of other lines or courses of action many negative 'actions' have only short-duration careers. I postponed writing the letter only from breakfast until mid-day; I rested from my climbing only for ten minutes; perhaps I held back my wound-ing repartee for only the few seconds before the quarrel ended. But still there was some path, a negative path, to which I delib-erately stuck, or else a primrose path in which I weakly, wearily or timorously dallied for a while, however short.

There seem to remain, however, some one-shot negative 'actions' which resist assimilation to lines or courses of action, however short. In order not to be drawn by our village Miss Bates into a chat which, on this occasion, would be embarras-sing, I stride past her in order to leave time only for a perfunc-tory 'Good morning'. (My *infra*-attempt to stride out might be thwarted by a pebble in my shoe; my *supra*-attempt to avoid a chat might be thwarted by her proving able while still conversing, to trot alongside me at my striding speed.) This omitting or failing to stop is not a duration-occupant. I would not use the continuous present tense or the imperfect tense in confessing it. It may be that this is just a special, because limiting, case of a line, namely not, as generally, a sequence of points, but just a single point. We noticed that while in general 'Not-x', for example 'Not at home', leaves nearly everything unparticularized, there are such limiting cases as 'Not-heads' which, in the context, is as determinate as 'Tails', and *vice versa*. So, in our village-context, 'Not-halting-for-a-chat' is as determinate as 'Walking-on' and 'Not-walking-on' as specific as 'Halting for a chat'. Either can be nominated as the negative of the other.

My *supra*-purpose does not, for once, govern a plurality of successive actual or possible *infra*-doings sharing with each other only a negative property; the statement of my purpose would be, apart from its single 'not', free of such quantifying, disjunctive and modal (etc.) expressions as 'whenever', 'never', 'some', 'can', 'must', 'may', etc. Roughly, in this particular context, there is only the singular and perfectly specific answer to the question, 'What *else* did I do than stop for a chat?', namely, indifferently, 'I strode on to avoid chatting' *or* 'To avoid chatting I omitted to halt'.

RESULTS

(1) We have solved or partly solved some teasers about what at first seemed to be negative actions. But as philosophers have not been much teased by these teasers, perhaps this result is only technically gratifying.

(2) The application to concepts of action, intention, etc. of certain notions of order-scaling which are already familiar inside the field of propoundables may serve to introduce some profitable diversifications, not only into the theory of doing, but also into the theory of saying.

(3) But, to put my cards on the table, our diagnosis of the factual hollowness of most of our negative 'actions', departing as it does equally – and similarly – from Cartesian as from

Behaviourist presumptions, may (but may not) open out into an enlargement of the 'mental' big enough to release and relieve some Cartesian genies. In some cases 'Not muscular because inner' may give place to 'Not muscular, because both *supra* and negative.

8

IMPROVISATION

We admire and envy people for, *inter alia*, their ability and readiness to innovate; especially so, of course, for the high qualities of some of their innovations. They may be only moderately or they may be exceptionally imaginative, inventive, enterprising, inquisitive, ingenious, witty, cunning, observant, responsive, alert or creative. It is characteristic of them that they compose, design, experiment, initiate, select, adapt, improvise, undertake, contrive, explore, parry, or speculate. What they do or say is apt to be slightly or highly original. They do not, all the time, just stick to the beaten tracks, to set routines or procedures, They are less creatures of habit than other people. Such folk need not be eccentric, crazy, frantic or silly. They may indeed be Heath Robinsons, but they may be Leonardo da Vincis; they may be jay-walkers, but they may be path-finders. It can be the good qualities of their wits and characters that come out in their impromptu jokes, their swift repartee, the fresh conclusions they draw, their shots at the goal or the ways they cope with traffic-emergencies. It is part of intelligence to seize new opportunities and to face new hazards; to be, in short, 'not a tram, but a bus'. What I am describing is not something that is peculiar to a few distinguished persons, but something that is shared in very different degrees in very different forms, and with very variable frequencies by all non-infantile, non-retarded, non-comatose human beings. I shall soon be reminding you of some of the familiar and unaugust sorts of improvisations which, just *qua* thinking beings, we all essay every day of the week, indeed in every hour of the waking day.

But first for two prefatory matters:

(A) I had originally intended to use the noun 'imagination' and the adjective 'imaginative' as general labels for the multifarious kinds that there are of inventiveness, creativeness, presence of mind, unhackneyedness, versatility, etc. But we are so used to associating imagination with the special activities of make-believe, which for our purposes are of only peripheral interest, that I shall not employ these particular labels very much. I shall also not rely much on the words 'original' and 'originality', since these have come to connote such summits of genius that we would usually credit with originality; Shakespeare, of course, but probably not Gilbert and Sullivan; Bach, but perhaps not Strauss; Galileo, but perhaps not Edison, and so on. Similarly the (to me repellent) words 'creativity' and 'creation' have been so monopolized by aestheticians that they have nothing like the wide coverage that I need. So I shall not try to find or requisition any one all-covering label, but shall just ring the changes, as I have already been doing, on such kindred but distinguishable verbs, adjectives, adverbs, etc., as 'experiment', 'compose', 'devise', 'witty', 'subtle', 'alert', 'ingeniously', 'enterprisingly', 'tactfully', and so on. Since it is our un-tram-likenesses in their widest variety that I want to discuss, we may gain more than we lose by doing without any single umbrella-label for them.

(B) Unfortunately the whole topic of originality has, until recently, been very wrongly neglected by epistemologists, I suppose for the bad, though potent, reason, that it has been quite rightly neglected by formal logicians. It has, until lately, been left chiefly to our aestheticians, enthusing about the special creativenesses (ugh!) of the most splendid artists, to press on us the correct and crucial point that, for example, verse-composition cannot be merely a well-drilled operation. If Wordworth's seventh sonnet had been a repetition of his sixth sonnet, it would not have been a new sonnet, and so not have been a new composition. Nor, in logic, can what I design be something that you have taught me.

Recently, however, Chomsky, perhaps following a lead from Wittgenstein's *Tractatus*, has rightly made much of the essential unmechanicalness of our quite ordinary conversings. The remark that I am engaged in making now is not, except some-times, the repetition of anything that I have heard or said before. It is, though usually a perfectly unsurprising remark, a fresh remark composed *ad hoc*, namely to fit a fresh conversational juncture. It does not come off an internal gramophone-record, or, when it does (as alas! it sometimes does, like my story of the big salmon that got away), then it is not a response to the momentary turn of the present conversation. Chomsky, how-

ever, in his praiseworthy zeal to take the clockwork out of
grammatical theory, tends to overlook our non-linguistic adroit-
nesses, improvisations, experimentations and, in a word, our
multifarious kinds of non-linguistic, as well as linguistic, 'Ad-
Hockery'. There is the cleverness of the caricaturist as well as the
cleverness of the conversationalist; the adroitness of the fencer
as well as that of the dialectical fencer.

My interest in the notions of imagination, invention, adven-
ture, improvisation, initiative, etc., derives from an interest in
the general notion or notions of *thinking*; i.e. in what it is that *Le
Penseur* is now doing which is beyond an infant, a reptile or a
clock. Unfortunately one over-dominant part of our everyday
ideas about such thinking is the assumption that since a stretch
of calculating, say, or translating or anagram-tackling certainly
does normally embody a succession of 'mental' moves, therefore
to think is, always and essentially, to go through a sequence of
'mental' leap-froggings. This step-after-step picture of cogitation is then apt, though not bound, to be hardened up into the
picture of a compulsory sequence of parade-ground steps indi-
vidually admitting of no spontaneity, selection, initiative or
imagination. On this assumption, whatever progress a thinker
has made, it is always proper to ask him not just How had he got
there? but via what interim paces had he marched from where
he had been to where he is now? Yet quite often, when we
ourselves are asked this How? question, we are completely
stumped for an answer. We can nominate no interim considerations at all. That impromptu but well-timed joke, that swift,
pertinent and unrehearsed reply to a question, that on-the-
spur-of-the-moment twist of the steering wheel – certainly we
had been awake and had used our wits; certainly we accept
blame or praise, applause or jeers, for the doing or saying, of it,
since it had been intentional and not a slip, an automatism, or a
seizure; certainly we had been thinking what we were saying or
doing, and minding how we said or did it. But to the request for
a chronicle of its component steps we have nothing to say,
except 'Oh, it just came to me', as if some thinking, including
some adequate or even bright thinking, is, after all, not a stage-
after-stage progression; or as if there could be the thinking-up of
a wanted something without the execution of any successive
pieces of thinking-out or thinking-over, however condensed or
swift.

Now if someone incautiously says 'Ladder-climbing always

requires the successive lifting of the feet up from one rung to a higher rung', he needs to be reminded 'And whence is the bottom rung mounted?' Or if someone improvidently says that the walker who crosses the stream by stepping from one stepping-stone to another must correspondingly step from each stepping-stone to the next via an intermediate stepping-stone, he too needs to be reminded that the very notion of a stepping-stone presupposes the possibility of running water being stepped straight *across*. In partial analogy I am arguing that some exercises of our wits, whether unsuccessful or successful, dull or bright, have got to be immediate and not mediated, direct engagings with once-only situations and not left-right, left-right progressions across a barrack-square. Certainly some of our thinking really is unmisleadingly, if over-picturesquely, describable as the taking of successive steps. But preoccupation with the successiveness of such steps makes us forget that each such step by itself may need for its individual description one or more of our epithets of un-tram-likeness. It must, if it is to be a positive move in a more-or-less consecutive train of thought, itself be experimental and/or apposite and/or bold and/or imaginative and/or wary, etc., unless their owner had not been thinking what he was saying or doing in the taking of that step, but had taken it from something like sheer habit or reflex or mimicry.

It may mitigate the initial strangeness of this idea that for some exercises of thought there are no processions of anything to be chronicled or charted, if we realize that to eliminate the favoured How? question is not to eliminate all questions. You must indeed not ask 'Off what still lower rung of the ladder did you mount its bottom rung?'; but you may still ask 'Meaning eventually to reach which branch of the tree? Expecting to scale how many higher rungs? Having had what practice with ladders? In obedience to, or defiance of, what instructions? Why so cautiously? Why bare-footed?, and so on. Similarly, my impromptu but pertinent reply to a surprising question is not rendered a mystery by the fact that 'It just came to me' without my taking any leap-frogging sub-steps, whether 'internal' or pencilled. Presence of mind on the road or in a conversation may incorporate no period of piecemeal mobilization, however short; but that does not require us to invoke such magical notions as those of an inspiration from one of the Nine Muses; or of a friendly or unfriendly interference by the Goddess of

Fortune; or even of the intervention of a contrived mental Faculty of Intuition.

I want now to adduce a perfectly general consideration which makes the occurrence of un-tram-like acts and responses on our part, or even on the part of animals, not rare things, but enormously frequent things. Despite what we are encouraged to believe about the Uniformity of Nature, in fact the vast majority of things that happen in the universe are in high or low degree unprecedented, unpredictable, and never to be repeated. They really are partly fortuitous. It can indeed be accurately predicted years ahead when it will be high tide at Dover on Christmas Day, such and such a year; but there is nothing from which it could be predicted that a particular seagull will (or else that it will not) be flying in a westerly direction over the largest tanker in the harbour just as the tide is turning on that day. To what branch of science would or could such a prediction belong? Tidology? Economics? Ornithology? or to a fortuitous collusion between the three of them? Fortuitous? It is sure enough that during the lunch-time rush-hour tomorrow pedestrians will have to wait for their chance to cross the High Street; but there is nothing from which even the City Police could predict that they will (or else that they will not) find a gap in the stream of vehicles opposite St. Mary's Church as the clock is striking one. If they do find such a gap, they will be slightly lucky. Yes, lucky. Circumstances, contingencies, opportunities and accidents are partly fortuitous concatenations of severally independent happenings and conditions. What comes to pass on one occasion has, with all its concomitants, origins and details, never taken place before and will never take place again. It may be and usually is completely unremarkable; as unsurprising when it happens as it had been unanticipated before it happened. The world and what occurs in it are, with a few exceptions, neither like a chaos nor yet like clockwork. We have to go for our suitable specimens of clockwork mostly to the starry heavens, the tides, the processes that are made or permitted to go on in laboratories and, of course, to the workings of clocks.

It follows that the things that we say and do in trying to exploit, avoid or remedy that small minority of the particular partly chance concatenations that happen to concern us cannot be completely pre-arranged. To a partly novel situation the response is necessarily partly novel, else it is not a response. The

fielder naturally expects that during the game some catches will
come his way; but he did not and could not make complete
preparations for just this particular catch, coming towards him
just where he now happens to be, with just this speed and
trajectory and at just this height above ground, and with him
himself having had just the thoughts and the intakes of breath
that he had been having. He has indeed learned from earlier
practice to make catches; but he could not, in logic, have been
trained to make just *this* catch. If, *per impossible*, he had been so
trained, then it would not have been *this* catch, but a different,
because prepared-for catch. His making it (or else his dropping
it) was a once-only seizing (or missing) of a once-only
opportunity, an opportunity that may indeed be quite like
opportunities that he has seized (or missed) before. But *this* one
(*qua* just *this* one) has not happened before and will not happen
again. Rather similarly, in a conversation or a debate, since what
I am to say to you next depends partly on how you are going to
complete your current sentence, I can harbour no internal 'tape'
already impressed with my impending remark or retort; nor,
usually, can you have already pre-plotted or rehearsed the final
development of the remark that you are now still in the middle
of composing-*cum*-delivering. Nonetheless, both of us will, if
challenged, nearly always admit or boast that we had certainly
thought up what to say, though only while we were actually in
the process of saying it. We had not been wandering or
parroting. What we said was, normally, what we then and there
wanted and meant to say; or if not, then we were ready to
correct it or apologize for it. So what we said was, for the most
part, a pertinent, *ad hoc* innovation. But it was said under the
latent and general governance of our previously acquired
phonetic, grammatical, stylistic and logical scruples, habits and
preferences. It was said in some degree heedfully; but this
adverb 'heedfully' does not connote the accompaniment of our
speaking by any ancillary acts of heed-paying. In my saying of
things that I never said before, I normally keep the
long-since mastered rules of English grammar without once
breaking the thread of my still developing remarks by
interposing grammarians' comments, corrections or
endorsements. Being on the *qui vive* against things going wrong,
far from requiring, requires *not* thinking commentators'
thoughts.

I want now to go further and to show that stepless though still innovative thinking is a necessary element even in inferring itself. Although the drawing of a conclusion from premises is our very paradigm of that step-after-step or leaplfrogging progression which we have hankered to impute to all thinking, yet this very leap-frogging process itself presupposes the presence of thinkings that are not themselves made up of leap-froggings. Consider the old story of the Parisian coffee-party. The ladies are listening with interest to their dear Abbé's reminiscences. At a certain point he tells them that his very first penitent had confessed to a murder. At that moment in walks a nobleman, who, after warmly greeting his old friend, the Abbé, tells the ladies that he had been the Abbé's first penitent. The ladies quickly draw the logically unassailable, though shocking, conclusion that the nobleman had once confessed to a murder. If asked afterwards whence they had got their new bit of scandal, they would have cited, *first,* the Abbé's item and *second* the nobleman's item of personal reminiscence. Neither item in the absence of the other would have carried the shocking implication. Neither the Abbé nor the nobleman had told the ladies, or even hinted to them, that the nobleman was a murderer.

We need to notice that the ladies were much helped to make their inference quickly, or even to make it at all, by the two very special circumstances, in which you and I and even Sherlock Holmes are hardly ever placed – (*a*) that the two bits of information happened to be presented to them in immediately consecutive moments; and (*b*) that both bits of information were of high gossip-interest. If the nobleman had not met the ladies on that day but only a week or two later, and if the Abbé's first penitent had confessed only to a distaste for hard work, the ladies would quite likely not have put the items together at all. Their prompt conclusion-drawing issued out of their synchronous cravings to know who had confessed to a murder, and what the nobleman had confessed. For, odd though it sounds, an inference can be logically necessary without it being necessary or even likely that anyone makes it – else detective work would be much easier than it is. Sherlock Holmes's conclusions were very far from forcing themselves instantaneously or even at all on Dr. Watson.

Let us suppose that the ladies answer satisfactorily our old

How? question, namely via what steps had they got to their shocking conclusion? They reply that the first they had been told about the first penitent's crime, and then they had been told who he was; or rather, to put in some safeguards, that first they had been told the first item, had heard it, had taken it in and had believed it; and that, second, they had heard, taken in and believed the second item. Fine; but now we want to know, Did they take in the Abbé's little story without thinking what they were hearing? Would they have made sense of it if they had been in a daze or a panic or thinking hard about something else, or even not been *au fait* with the Abbé's peculiar French dialect? No, of course they had attended to the Abbé's story; they had given their French-trained ears and anecdote-trained minds to it. They had not just uncomprehendingly heard some vocal noises, alongside some traffic noises from the street. But if their taking in this story had involved their thinking, then of what ulterior steps or leap-froggings had *this* consisted? Off what lower rung did the climber step up on to the bottom rung? Via what intervening stepping-stone did the walker step from the bank to the first stepping-stone? Or from this stone to its successor?

Look now at the conclusion-end of the ladies' inference. Perhaps a couple of the ladies are too devoted to the nobleman to relish the idea that he had committed a murder. So for a short time they reluctantly and suspiciously entertain this shocking idea, while still hoping to find a flaw in the argument that threatened to prove it via the two premises. In considering the implication as something which may still be rejectable, they are indubitably thinking; indeed, maybe they actually voice what they are thinking in such words as; 'Our dear Marquis commit a murder? Never!' In *this* suspicious thinking there need be no ulterior premise-assembling; nothing to give anchorage to our old question, 'Via what subsidiary steps?' So that very thinking that really does embody considered steps leading to a considered conclusion presupposes considerings that do not in their turn embody passages from steps via steps to steps. And these unchainlike considerings will nesessarily be characterizable as, for example, tentative, circumspect, fanciful, apposite or rebellious.

From all this, a quite general lesson proffers itself. If *Le Penseur* is on a certain occasion thinking, then (*a*) he must be engaging himself, quite likely vainly, erroneously or inefficiently, in an at least partly fresh contingency. He is in however modest a degree and however perfunctorily being exploratory and/or experimental and/or enterprising, etc. or else he is not applying his wits to just *this* contingency. But (*b*) he must be, in some measure, exploiting on this once-only particular contingency some general lessons previously learned and not since totally forgotten. Else he is not paying to the situation any degree of heed, and so is not minding what he is doing or saying, or how he is doing or saying it. Like a parrot or a delirious man, perhaps, he is just uttering noises that are not, unless accidentally, words of a language; and his noise-sequences are not, unless accidentally, what grammar admits. Being unalive to the risk of error and failure, he neither withdraws nor corrects anything he utters. Or, being unalive to the risk of collisions or skids, he spins the steering-wheel wildly or just as wildly leaves it to manage itself. No, to be thinking what he is here and now up against, he must both be trying to adjust himself to just this present once-only situation *and* in doing this to be applying lessons already learned. There must be in his response a union of some Ad Hockery with some know-how. If he is not at once *improvising* and improvising *warily*, he is not engaging his somewhat trained wits in some momentarily live issue, but perhaps acting from sheer unthinkable habit. So thinking, I now declare quite generally, is, at the least, the engaging of partly trained wits in a partly fresh situation. It is the pitting of an acquired competence or skill against unprogrammed opportunity, obstacle or hazard. It is a bit like putting some *new* wine into *old* bottles.

Before concluding I just air an objection that will rightly be made. Quite often a person is confronted by a problem which he has often tackled before without any success. Perhaps he is battering his head against an old philosophical obstacle or against a stubborn anagram. So where is that fresh, once-only contingency with which he is, on this account of mine, trying to cope? Well, his first, second and twentieth bangs on the inhospitable door had differed from his twenty-first bang at least in this. This new bang, unlike any of them, is his twenty-*first* bang. His problem is a slightly more· familiar problem than it had been last time; his present bang, though very likely still unsuccessful, may be, in its direction or vehemence, or whatever, a slightly experimental variation on its predecessors. But even when he can give to his twenty-first bang no fresh impetus, no untried angle of approach, no new twist of any sort, he may still make that same old approach in the new hope, sometimes realized, that *this time* a stroke of sheer luck may cause *this* bang to achieve something that had not been achieved by its predecessors. So he is a little readier than last time to notice the preacher's use of a word sharing a yet untried something with his anagram. Or he re-mutters the words of his still unsatisfactory argument not wholly mechanically but in the new hope, occasionally realized, that their very boringness may irritate him into trying out an alternative phrase or a fresh word-order with a bit of new life in it. His question has not changed since last time, but *he* may have changed. The very same tree that Tommy could not climb last year is climbed by him this year because his legs and arms are longer. So, not indeed the tree, but his task has changed. Thus too the thinker, the converser or the fencer is himself, in some measure, a once-only factor in his own once-only situations. It would be absurd to command him 'Think again *exactly* what you thought last time'; 'Repeat *without any change at all* your experiment of last time'. The command itself would be a fresh influence. To obey it would be to disobey it.

APPENDIX:

ON BOUWSMA'S WITTGENSTEIN

Like us, Bouwsma has his own Wittgenstein.

(1) He ends by assimilating the Wittgenstein of the *Philosophical Investigations* to the psychoanalyst. Now Wittgenstein did at one stage ply this model. But the *Investigations,* outside 254–255 and perhaps 133, does not use it. Moreover, for Bouwsma himself the *Investigations* is a manual of philosophical skills; but abilities to extricate oneself from conceptual tangles are acquired sagacities, not convalescences.

(2) The *Investigations* does indeed coach us in the arts of conceptual disentanglement. Its accents are occasionally quite governessy. But Bouwsma forgets that behind the mentor there was the philosopher. The knots which Wittgenstein shows us how to untie are knots which he himself had first to find out how to untie. It is the *Notebooks* especially that exhibit to us the philosopher eagerly or despondently exploring his own flybottles from inside. For those undocile souls who respond less emulously to solicitous shepherdings than to live examples of pioneering, Bouwsma should have vouchsafed something about Wittgenstein the explorer. Though we hear much of our warfare against confusions, no particular pocket of confusion gets pinpointed, or the appropriate way of conquering it specified.

We are told with pathos that Wittgenstein 'sought to bring relief, control, calm, quiet, peace, release, a certain power.' Well! – what of the Wittgenstein who got us interested, fascinated, excited, angry, shocked? He electrified us. Whom did he ever tranquillize?

(3) Like Wittgenstein, Bouwsma shudders at the idea that the philosopher has theories. Very well, let us relinquish to the Royal Society this vulgar noun. But Bouwsma's primness gets the better of him when he, abetted by Wittgenstein, says of the

Philosophical Investigations, '. . . not at all as a theory of mind, in
fact as no theory at all. . . . It contains no arguments at all. There
are no proofs. It rectifies nothing. There is nothing to rectify.
There are no refutations. . . .' Later, he prefers the phrase 'the art
of discover[ing] and dispelling confusions', to the coarser
locution 'the correction of mistakes'. No theory of mind? No
refutations or corrections of mistakes? Yet Wittgenstein often
declares that quite definite mistakes had been committed by St.
Augustine, Russell, and the author of the *Tractatus
Logico-Philosophicus.* Nothing to rectify? Yet Bouwsma quotes,
'The philosopher's treatment of a question is like the treatment
of an illness' (255). No arguments? Not even arguments about
the privacy of sensations versus the imputed privacy of
sensation-concepts? No arguments? Yet, 'That is to confound
the meaning of a name with the bearer of the name. When Mr.
N. N. dies one says that the bearer of the name dies, not that the
meaning dies. And it would be nonsensical to say that, for (*denn*) if
the name ceased to have meaning it would make no sense to say
Mr. N. N. is dead' (40).

No arguments? Yet, 'You say the point isn't the word, but its
meaning, and you think of the meaning as a thing (*Sache*) of the
same kind as the word, though also different from the word.
Here the word, there the meaning (*Bedeutung*). The money and
the cow that you can buy with it. (But contrast, the money and
its use.)' (120).

No arguments? Yet, 'I remember having meant (*gemeint*) *him*.
Am I remembering a process or state? – When did it begin, what
was its course, etc.?' (661).

No arguments? But lots of Wittgenstein's wearisome
interrogatives are, like this last one, the rhetorically barbed
conclusions of *reductio ad absurdum* arguments.

The clang of Wittgenstein's metal against the metals of Frege,
Russell, Ramsey, Brouwer, Moore, and the author of the
Tractatus is here muted to a soothing bedside murmur.

INDEX